W9-AZS-846

HOW TO
MAKE
FRIENDS

A Lucky Duck Book

HOW TO MAKE FRIENDS

Building Resilience and Supportive Peer Groups

RUTH MacCONVILLE

Macquarie Regional Library

Los Angeles • London • New Delhi • Singapore

© Ruth MacConville 2008

First published 2008

Apart from any fair dealing for the purposes of research or private study, or criticism or review, as permitted under the Copyright, Designs and Patents Act, 1988, this publication may be reproduced, stored or transmitted in any form, or by any means, only with the prior permission in writing of the publishers, or in the case of reprographic reproduction, in accordance with the terms of licences issued by the Copyright Licensing Agency. Enquiries concerning reproduction outside those terms should be sent to the publishers.

All material on the accompanying CD-ROM can be printed off and photocopied by the purchaser/user of the book. The CD-ROM itself may not be reproduced in its entirety for use by others without prior written permission from SAGE. The CD-ROM may not be distributed or sold separately from the book without the prior written permission of SAGE. Should any one wish to use the materials from the CD-ROM for conference purposes they would require separate permission from SAGE.

The right of the author to be indentified as Author of this work has been asserted by him/her in accordance with the Copyright, Design and Patents Act 1988.

SAGE Publications Ltd
1 Oliver's Yard
55 City Road
London EC1Y 1SP

SAGE Publications Inc.
2455 Teller Road
Thousand Oaks, California 91320

SAGE Publications India Pvt Ltd
B 1/I 1 Mohan Cooperative Industrial Area
Mathura Road
New Delhi 110 044

SAGE Publications Asia-Pacific Pte Ltd
33 Pekin Street #02-01
Far East Square
Singapore 048763

Library of Congress Control Number: 2008925101

British Library Cataloguing in Publication data

A catalogue record for this book is available from the British Library

ISBN 978-1-4129-2256-2

Typeset by C&M Digitals (P) Ltd., Chennai, India
Printed in India at Replika Pvt. Ltd
Printed on paper from sustainable resources

Contents

Acknowledgements

I would l ike to thank the children and young people who have shared with me their experiences of making friends and who have been my inspiration throughout. Without them this book could not have been written.

I would also like to thank the many parents and practitioners I have worked with over the years who have taught me so much about children who struggle to make friends.

Thanks also to SAGE and especially to George Robinson who has always been available for helpful advice and provided invaluable encouragement throughout.

Finally, thanks to family and friends for their patience while I worked on this book.

Introduction and background

Without good enough peer relationships children and young people are psychologically at risk. It is generally agreed among parents and educators that peer relationships provide a unique and essential contribution to pupils' emotional and social development.

Children who are accepted by their peers are likely to thrive whereas those who suffer rejection often become increasingly isolated. Children and young people need a minimum level of acceptance by their peer group. Peer relationships matter and are of developmental significance. Harris (1998) concluded, based on a review of the literature, that peer relationships are of primary importance in the development of psychological well-being. Interest in peer relations has burgeoned in recent years and there has been an increasing emphasis on the business of building emotional resilience and encouraging children and young people to get along with others. Goleman (1995) emphasises the value of social and emotional learning and links emotional intelligence to success in all domains of life. There is now growing evidence that academic learning itself is improved when social and emotional matters are explicitly addressed (Petrides et al., 2004). The impact of emotional literacy is that instead of being at the mercy of our emotions we can use our thinking to reflect upon them, shape them and moderate them. The development of emotional literacy therefore can help us improve our motivation, thinking skills and our thinking can help us to become more emotionally literate.

This evidence lifts social and emotional learning firmly out of the 'deficit' model of this work and solely as a response to children and young people with social , emotional and behavioural difficulties (SEBD) into the mainstream arena. The promotion of the 'Social and Emotional aspects of Learning' (SEAL) cross curriculum materials (DfES, 2005) as an entitlement curriculum for *all* children confirms this change of status, as do references to the domains of emotional literacy in the Primary National Strategy (PNS). Putting in place a taught curriculum focusing on social and emotional learning within a school ethos that values and consolidates this work can therefore have significant outcomes.

This programme targets the whole class and takes a proactive approach to the business of building emotional resilience and encouraging children and young people to get along with others. A priority agenda over the past decade has been that of inclusion which also has specific links with the emotional and social aspects of learning. Children and young people who struggle to access learning for a wide variety of reasons can become disaffected. Hart (1996) has emphasised that in most schools collaboration between pupils and therefore effective group work does not take place.

Pupils are rarely taught the principles of effective co-operation. Being able to work effectively as part of a group is however a critical skill in all contexts – school, life and work (Goleman, 1998).

Emphasising the celebration of diversity, acceptance and building the skills of empathy can do a great deal to facilitate inclusion and support the outcomes of the Every Child Matters agenda (DfES, 2003).

- Be Healthy: The programme encourages friendships across the peer group and enables children to recognise that they are accepted and liked by their peers.

- Stay Safe: The activities and scenarios contained in the programme challenge pupils to explore and change their attitude to discrimination and bullying and to view the possible consequences of both their attitudes and actions through others eyes.

- Enjoy and Achieve: The programme emphasises fun combined with achievement. All the activities are interactive and provide positive feedback. Pupils are encouraged throughout the programme to look for recognition of their achievements within themselves.

- Make a Positive Contribution: The programme emphasises positive relationships and respect and acceptance of others.

A central aim of this programme then is to support the development of positive working relationships between pupils and enable them to build friendly connections with each other so that friendships can develop. This aim is identified in the National Curriculum Statement of Values:

We value relationships as fundamental to the development and fulfilment of ourselves and others, and to the good of the community.

The programme contributes to the development of four of the key skills which are embedded in the National Curriculum. These are communication, working with others, improving own learning and performance and problem solving. The programme also specifically addresses skills which have their basics in the friendship box. These include active listening, the ability to take turns and share, knowing how and when to apologise, how to problem solve and resolve conflict, how to manage being teased. A unique feature of the programme is that it addresses the development of nonverbal communication skills; the ability to read social cues.

The Development of Friendships

The majority of us have groups of friends that may change slowly over the course of our lives. Beginning a new job, moving house, becoming parents are frequently the time when new friendships are forged. Most of us take these relationships for granted and expect them to happen as a natural course of events. Parents also usually take it for granted that their children will automatically make friends when they go to school. For some children this is not the case. These children frequently experience feelings of isolation and loneliness. The essential question 'How do we go about making friends?' is not an easy one to answer but it is an important question nonetheless because those who are able to make friends are most likely to be happy and fulfilled and those who are unable to get along with others are likely to be, at best, lonely.

Newspapers all too frequently feature items about children and young people who have been somehow unable to get along with their peers and have ended up isolated and bullied. A common theme in these nearly all of these accounts is the pain and bewilderment that is expressed by parents when they discover that their child has been bullied:

You go from anger to despair to wanting to provide a more protective framework for your child. (Times Educational Supplement, 13 May 2005)

It's not easy and research confirms that parents experience great difficulty responding appropriately to their child's social dilemmas. Staff in schools also often express bewilderment that despite taking the appropriate measures and using the full range of strategies that are available to them they have not managed to salvage the situation. The bottom line is that watching children and young people suffer socially is very hard to bear. Children, however usually fear that adult interventions will make things worse. They have a point. On the whole the less *direct* adult involvement there is in friendships the more children will learn about each other and themselves. A parent or member of staff may advise a child to find a different friend but children that advice is not usually followed. The reality is that children are likely to spend a great deal of time in each other's company away from adult supervision. Unbeknown to the adult the friendship may be very important even when it is seemingly, from an adult perspective, it is very out of balance.

The social problems of children present us with a paradox. Although we cannot intervene directly in situations there is a huge role for us to play in shaping the social abilities of children. We can improve a child's social destiny by acknowledging the weight of social power in children's lives and concentrating our efforts on providing opportunities for children to connect with others, teach and model prosocial behaviours and support their friendships.

Making friends and keeping them is one of the most critical tasks we face as human beings. Children need to learn that it takes time, effort and most importantly knowledge and skills to do well. Nowicki and Duke (1996) emphasise that most of what goes into being successful at getting along with others is learned. This learning firstly takes place in the home and happens through modelling and teaching and it is later applied outside the home with play-mates and then peers in school. Children of different ages possess different capacities for developing social relationships with their peers.

Stages of Friendship Development

2–3 year olds

This is the time for enjoying parallel play, children learn to enjoy being in each other's company. These social contexts resemble harmonious mother-child dyads. At this stage children are beginning to learn limits and are listening to language from each other. At this stage children are entirely dependent upon their parents for contact with their peers and this contact is usually characterized by a sense of goodwill and trust that re-creates the harmonious mother-child dyad.

3–6 year olds

This is the time for trying out aggression, boys tend towards horseplay wrestling and rolling around on floor, they threaten with fists and learn about their own aggression. Girls tend to tease each other. There is an emphasis on children appreciating each other for the material benefits that an association can generate, for example children will want to play with the child who has an interesting toy or something good to eat. The adult's role at this stage is to be sure there are opportunities for children to be together and play and relate to each other. If a child is isolated staff and parents should take it very seriously and seek help. This is the time to learn serious lessons in give and take with others. Research suggests that a spoiled or over-protected child won't make it.

6–9 year olds

At this stage children begin to learn to appreciate each other for personal qualities rather than the material benefits of an association. Children begin to form close friendships and can be devastated when they are deserted for another. Boys form small gangs and have one or two close friends with whom they must be all the time. Girls also need small groups. Within these groups children exclude, woo and bully. The parents role is to respect these close friendships, even though they may not approve of some of the provocative play, bullying and teasing. It is a critical time for every child to learn about himself. Children will learn how to live up to the demands of closeness and form deep friendships.

9–12 year olds

At this stage friends continue to be playmates but over time friendship takes on a deeper level of meaning than just having fun. Children begin to differentiate between between friends (who have a greater sense of one another's needs and capacities) and companions who one is happy to spend time with but not necessarily close to. At this stage children may also develop a close mutual friendship with a same-sex peer. Sullivan (1952) coined the term *chum* to describe this sort of relationship. Chumship wrote Sullivan offers children the first opportunity to see oneself through other's eyes and experience intimacy. It plays a powerful developmental function as it shapes one's sense of self worth and sense of self. It provides a forum for overcoming bad experiences and provides validation of one's interests, hopes and fears. Chumship helps you to learn to be sensitive to others and provides the sort of support that parents cannot provide.

It is important to recognise that social skills and friendship are not the same thing. It may be helpful to think in terms of social skills being the foundation on which friendships may develop whereas poor social skills can make it almost impossible for a relationship to grow. Social skills are a critical but not a sufficient foundation for friendships to develop. Reciprocity, commitment, giving and sharing are the essential components of friendship (Hartup, 1992). These qualities however cannot be taught. A child has to bring a sense of confidence and trust to a relationship in order for it to become a friendship.

It has been argued that teaching relationship skills is perhaps the most critical area of education. Children are likely to learn successfully if their basic physical needs are met, they feel unthreatened and valued and have a sense of belonging to the group. Respect is the mantra. Children and young people who bring a wide range of social skills to their interactions are more likely to get along with others and make friends. In order to gain acceptance from their peers children must be able to seek out others and be agreeable to them when asked to do something reasonable. Pupils who give others a large number of positive responses are more likely to be chosen as friends. Communication and listening skills are also important. Children who are poor communicators more likely to be rejected or ignored. Pupils skilled in initiating conversations have more friends. Significant shyness or not knowing how to make positive approaches towards other children will inhibit the development of friendship. The ability to control aggression is also a key skill in social attractiveness. Disrupting the activities of other children or initiating unprovoked physical or verbal attacks are major factors in being disliked

The quality of peer relationships is a good indicator of a child's healthy development. A child who is isolated in school or shunned may be transmitting subtle messages to other children of anxiety, self-doubt, turmoil to which adults may not be sensitive. Children will not usually accept these struggles in their peers as they find it too threatening. If parents suspect that their child is being rejected they should take it as a warning that their child is unhappy. If a child is acutely upset because of for example a bereavement or loss, other children will probably be sympathetic, understanding, protective as long as child retains basic ability for making relationships underneath the pain and turmoil. Children can usually distinguish between a child who has suffered a loss or who is temporarily upset and one who is isolated because of deep-seated social problems.

The programme should not be considered as a stand-alone attempt by the school to enhance the emotional resilience and co-operation of its pupils. It should rather be viewed as a valuable piece of a jigsaw of provision which also includes a robust behaviour policy, committed staff and a variety of peer support programmes.

The structure of the programme

The course consists of 26 sessions each of which focuses on an aspect of building emotional resilience. The sessions aim to raise pupil's awareness and understanding of a range of interpersonal skills, develop their ability to communicate with each other and work more effectively together. It also aims to contribute to the development of specific thinking skills:

- information-processing

- reasoning

- enquiry

- creative thinking

- evaluation skills.

Goleman (1998) emphasises that the most effective learning opportunities for developing social, emotional and behavioural skills must involve participative, experiential and interactive activities which enable individuals to engage at a personal level and to construct their own understanding. 'The process of becoming emotionally literate as an individual or as an organisation must engage both hearts and minds' (Morris and Casey, 2006, p. xix).

Central to the programme is a solution focused approach (Rhodes and Ajmal, 1995) which means that any discussion is forward thinking, positive in outlook and committed to finding new ways of addressing difficult issues. A range of helpful approaches associated with a solution focused approach are introduced throughout the programme. Each session contains resources for organising whole-class lessons in ways which have been shown to improve the quality of pupil's co-operation with each other and their active participation in the class. The final two sessions of the programme 'Y is for You' and 'Z is for Zest for Living' do not follow the format of the other sessions. Y is for You involves each pupil in a personal evaluation of the programme and the identification of specific goals for future learning. Z is for Zest for Living provides an opportunity for pupils to demonstrate their learning throughout the course by coming together in a session which is devoted to a celebration of the end of the programme. During this final session certificates are distributed to each child. The purpose of the certificates is to emphasise to each pupil what they have achieved in their efforts to co-operate and get along together during the programme. A suggested format for the certificate is included on page 142.

The sessions are arranged in the sequence of the alphabet.

Notes for teachers

'How to make friends' is intended as an approach to teaching and learning as well as a set of specific activities. An interactive teaching style in which the teacher encourages pupils to contribute to discussion is central to this programme. Using open–ended questions for which there are neither right or wrong answers will encourage pupils to contribute. Paraphrasing and scaffolding pupils' contributions and reflecting back what they are saying will ensure that pupils feel listened to and that their ideas are valued. Another advantage of paraphrasing is that pupils' contributions can be expanded into more appropriate language. This is important as an overall aim of the programme is to enable pupils to develop an enhanced vocabulary for expressing how they feel and communicating with others.

The sessions can be delivered in a variety of ways, with a whole class or with a small group. They can also be used as part of the PHSE or citizenship curriculum. The sessions do not have to be delivered in sequence, it may be useful to use a session in response to a specific classroom or school situation however it will be important to introduce A is for Attitude as the first session in order to set the tone for developing collaboration and exploratory talk which can be emphasised during subsequent sessions.

Link to Classroom Activities

It is an important that the skills and behaviours that are emphasised throughout the programme such as for example paying compliments become an integral part of classroom activities and that pupils do not always look to adults to receive positive feedback. Pupils need to receive compliments from their peers as well. Circle Time, for example, can provide an opportunity for pupils to be encouraged to say one nice thing about a classmate. Circle Time can also be used to encourage pupils to share something about themselves that they feel proud of. The ability to reflect one's own performance and achievements is an important part of the development of one's sense of self and achievement.

A positive classroom can be encouraged by staff rewarding co-operation between peers and the social skill of praise. A chart which records when staff notice pupils saying something positive to a classmate or doing something helpful for a peer without being asked can be a source of encouragement to all. The teacher may wish to reward the whole class when the chart shows a certain number of positive responses.

An important component of this session has been to encourage pupils to recognise their existing social strengths and the different sorts of relationships that they have already built at home and in school. Teaching pupils to recognise their own social strengths is essential and staff can encourage pupils' feelings of accomplishment by the way in which they praise pupils. For example praise such as 'You must feel proud of yourself for inviting all those children to join in the game at playtime' or 'You must be very happy that you were able to help (name of child) work with others in the group'. Encouraging children and young people to look inside themselves for self-approval rather than wait passively for praise from others can significantly improve the self-esteem of individual pupils and the overall social climate of the classroom.

Self-Approval

An important component of the programme is encouraging pupils to feel good about themselves and enable them to look inside themselves for self-approval. Teaching children and young people to recognise their own achievements is vital in large and busy classrooms where pupils may have to wait to receive praise from staff. As this programme has been designed to build on pupils existing strengths and prosocial behaviours it is likely that an increasing number of pupils will respond to questions that the teacher poses to the whole group or class. When a large number of pupils seek to answer a question those who do not get selected to respond can feel left out or even despondent. As this programme relies on pupils' individual responses rather than 'right' or 'wrong' answers it is essential that the teachers acknowledge the contributions of *all* pupils including those pupils who have not been selected to answer. One way of addressing this issue is for the teacher to say to the class 'All those children who had a good idea, well done and pat yourself on the back for putting your hand up with an answer'. When time permits it can also be helpful to then allow these pupils to share their idea for a few moments with the person next to them.

An Inclusive Approach

Children and young people often react to difficult situations in ineffective ways by either becoming angry and lashing out at others or by becoming withdrawn and passive. Such responses do not enable the pupils to find manageable solutions for their difficulties. Teachers have a key role to play in teaching pupils positive ways of managing difficult situations and how to evaluate which solutions are better and more likely to lead to positive consequences. Providing *all* pupils with a thinking strategy which reduces the risk of pupils developing ongoing peer relationship problems is an essential component of developing a positive classroom environment in which interpersonal difficulties are unlikely to accelerate. Including pupils who have social and behavioural difficulties or at risk of developing them in the programme minimises the risk of them experiencing social rejection by being singled out for specific teaching. An inclusive approach promotes classroom social cohesion and empathy amongst *all* pupils.

Neglected Children

Happily the majority of children are liked and accepted by their peers. They have positive qualities, which make them liked by their peers and their acceptance by their classmates reinforces their positive attributes. Being left out however can be a particular problem for some pupils who have very little social impact in the classroom and are neglected by their peers. Children with sensory impairment often fall into this category of 'neglected children' as they find the to and fro of conversation, particularly group conversation almost impossible to follow and non-verbal clues such as facial expression, eye contact may not be available to them. Thompson (et al., 2001) suggests that though the social suffering of this neglected children is real, their pain may not come to anybody's attention as they tend not to act out their difficulties. Although the programme sets out to teach pupils a set of specific social skills and is not intended to be therapeutic intervention sessions Teachers need to be aware that sessions such as' Left out' for example may trigger a powerful response in some children. Look out therefore for pupils who may seem distressed or withdrawn after a session and remind pupils at the end of each session that if they have any worries or concerns they should talk to a member of staff.

The structure of the sessions

Resources

Materials needed for each session are as follows:

- Approximately 45 minutes to run each session.

- A3 copy of session poster.

- A4 copies of session poster for each pupil.

- A4 copies of activity sheets for each pupil.

- Pair and Share evaluation sheet for each pupil.

- Pens, pencils, rubbers, sharpeners etc.

- Friendship Logs.

The last two sessions follow a slightly different format so the resources for these are listed on the relevant pages. Each session has a copiable poster illustrating the relevant letter of the alphabet and an activity sheet. The posters provide the initial teaching points for each session. It is helpful for the teacher to enlarge the posters to a A3 size and use them as focal points for the lesson by placing them on a flip chart or white board. Each lesson also has an activity sheet and a copy of the Pair and Share review form is also required for each pupil.

A time allocation of approximately 45 minutes is suggested for each session however this may be extended or reduced according to the size of the group.

The Friendship Log

Each pupil should be provided with their own individual Friendship Log, an A4 folder in which they can keep a record of the sessions. A record form, which contains a list of the sessions is included for this purpose. Pupils should be encouraged to store their own individual copies of the poster for each session, which they can personalise and also copies of the activity sheet which is completed during each session.

The Friendship Log allows each individual pupil to build up their own folder of work associated with the programme. It is important that pupils are encouraged to take a pride in their Log and add to it with their own personal thoughts and also with cuttings from magazines and newspapers which are relevant to the programme. Take Away Activities are suggested at the end of each session. The Friendship Log also provides pupils with a vehicle in which they can ask the teacher questions about the sessions and to which the teacher can respond with comments, stickers and personal words of encouragement for individual pupils. Thus the Friendship Log allows the teacher to have a more personal dialogue with each pupil about the programme.

It is important to ensure that pupils who experience difficulties with literacy are not penalised. Thus encouraging pupils to express themselves in the Friendship Log through the use of pictures, drawings and mind maps is important as well as the availability of adult assistance to scribe pupils' views or help with spellings.

It is essential that the creativity and individuality of each Friendship Log is fully celebrated.

The Friendship Log can also be used to store any additional work relevant to the programme that the pupils choose to complete between sessions.

Whole Class Introduction

Aims
A critical aspect of the programme is that each session starts with the teacher clearly explaining the aims of the session to the pupils. This is important in order to create a shared purpose and keep the focus firmly on the theme of the session.

The teacher then explains the main focus of the lesson. The introductory notes for each session are written as guidance notes for teachers. In some sessions an illustrative script is also included. At the end of this first phase of the session the teacher should fully explain the activity which the pupils are expected to complete in the 'Pair and Share' middle phase of the session.

Pair and Share
During this second phase of the lesson the pupils work in random pairs that the pupils 'self-select' via a pairing exercise. There are many ways in which pupils can be paired however whichever way the teacher chooses it is important that pupils succeed easily in finding a partner. One of the most effective ways of pairing pupils is for each child to write their names on a piece of card or draw their own portrait and label it with their name prior to the the first session. The teacher then distributes these name cards or portraits to each pupil randomly at each subsequent session or sets them out face downwards on a table for pupils to select thus determining their choice of who will be their partner for the session. It is important that pupils are able to easily select another card if they have previously worked with a child. Once pupils have 'found' their

partner the expectation must be that they sit together and commence the activity in partnership. The need to be 'with' each other rather than just sitting by each other must be encouraged by emphasising positive body language and also effective listening and speaking skills.

Sometimes the teacher may decide to partner a particular pupil with a teaching assistant for a particular activity to enable the the child to receive adult modelling of sharing and co-operative behaviour. In such circumstances it is important that the teacher removes that particular pupil's name or portrait from the class set to avoid confusion when the pupils are selecting partners.

During 'Pair and Share' the pupils are given a short activity to complete. All of the activities are easily achievable so that there is an inbuilt element of success for each partnership. This is important as working in partnership successfully together means that pupils are more likely to get to know each other and make friends. Activity sheets are included for each session.

It is essential that the teacher is busy during the the 'Pair and Share' phase of the lesson. Walking around the classroom and providing vigilant monitoring and visual and auditory scanning is key to effective classroom management. Firstly the teacher can praise the pupils as they work in partnership with each other by identifying and highlighting good practice. Secondly, the teacher can catch problems early and can stop and assist pupils as necessary by encouraging reluctant partners and being aware of the specific needs of partnerships which are likely to be volatile. This will prevent frustration on the part of many pupils and provide recognition and encouragement for their learning efforts.

When the Pair and Share activity is completed pupils are encouraged to give positive feedback to their partner about how they have enjoyed working together and then complete a Pair and Share review form which they then store in their Friendship Log.

It is essential that pupils conclude their time with each other in a friendly and positive manner. The overall success of the programme and its contribution to creating a positive climate within the classroom will depend upon the level of good will and co-operation which is shared by each member of the class.

Final Plenary

The final part of each session is the time when the teacher brings the whole class together in order to review the learning and co-operation that has taken place. Encouraging pupils to reflect upon their own learning can help them to pinpoint steps of achievement as they occur. It is envisaged that pupils will increasingly learn to value their achievements and enjoy a growing awareness of their learning throughout the sessions. The aim is to enable pupils to look within themselves for confirmation of their learning. By reflecting on their own work and learning process pupils can:

- enjoy a greater awareness of what they have learnt

- understand the purpose of the sessions

- set themselves realistic targets

- gain self-esteem through pride in accomplishment.

In practical terms the final plenary of each session is a time when the teacher can:

- enable pupils to share their work with the class

- lead a class discussion, emphasising the main learning points which have emerged

- review the lesson aims, allowing the class to consider whether they have been fulfilled.

It is essential to finish each session on a positive note. It is suggested that the teacher asks the class at the end of each session whether they consider the group has achieved its aims.

The teacher should model co-operative and respectful behaviour throughout the programme and each session should end with a formal thank you from the teacher to the class.

Take Away Activities

Each of the sessions include a list of activities for the pupils to work on either independently at the end of the lesson or later at home. The main aim of the Take Away Activities is to encourage the pupils to think about the sessions and evaluate their progress in developing their interpersonal skills throughout the programme and in their own time. Pupils should be encourage to follow up classroom work at home and develop their understanding of the concepts introduced in the sessions by reading, watching TV and films and by being generally observant. It is suggested that the list of Take Away Activities that is provided for for each session are placed in a prominent place in the classroom so that pupils can refer to them during the week. Alternatively the teacher may wish to provide pupils with individual copies of the Take Away Activities that accompanies each session.

The lesson plans can be used as a template for developing further lessons.

References

DfES (2003) *Every Child Matters*, London, DfES.

DfES (2005) *Excellence and Enjoyment: Social and emotional aspects of learning (SEAL)* 0110–2008G, London, DfES.

Goleman, D. (1995) *Emotional Intelligence: Why it can matter more than IQ*. New York, Bantam Books.

Goleman, D. (1998) *Working with Emotional Intelligence*. New York, Bantam Books.

Harris, J.R. (1998) *The Nurture Assumption,* New York, Free Press.

Hart, S. (1996) *Beyond Special Needs*, London, Paul Chapman Publishing.

Hartup, R. (1992) Conflict and friendship relations, in C.U. Shanz and W. W. Hartup (eds) *Conflict in Child and Adolescent Development,* Cambridge, Cambridge University Press.

Morris, E. and Casey, J. (2006) *Developing Emotionally Literate Staff,* London, Paul Chapman Publishing.

Nowicki, S. (2000) How to make friends, in M.P. Duke and S.B. Duke (eds) *What Works with Children: Wisdom and reflections from people who have devoted their careers to kids*. Atlanta, Peachtree Publishers.

Nowicki, S. and Duke, M.P. (1996) *Teaching Your Child the Language of Social Success,* Atlanta, Peachtree Publishers.

Petrides, K.V., Mischel, W. and Peake, P.K. (2004) The role of trait emotional intelligence in academic performance and deviant behaviour at school, *Personality and Individual Differences*, 36: 277–293.

Rhodes, J. and Ajmal, Y. (1995) *Solution Focused Thinking in Schools*, London, Brief Therapy Publications.

Sullivan, H.S. (1952) *The Interpersonal Theory of Psychiatry*, New York, Norton.

Thompson, M., O'Neill Grace, C. with Cohen, L.J. (2001) *Best Friends, Worst Enemies: Children's friendships, popularity and social cruelty*, London, Penguin, Michael Joseph.

Record Form for Friendship Log
How to make friends

	Date	Partner	Mark out of 10	Take away activities
Session 1 A is for Attitude				
Session 2 B is for Bounce Back				
Session 3 C is for Compliments				
Session 4 D is for Different				
Session 5 E is for Empathy				
Session 6 F is for Fair				
Session 7 G is for Get Over It				
Session 8 H is for Help Yourself				
Session 9 I is for Invitations				
Session 10 J is for Joining In				
Session 11 K is for Keep Your Word				
Session 12 L is for Left Out				
Session 13 M is for Managing Moods				
Session 14 N is for Nice Ways of Saying No				
Session 15 O is for Open Up				
Session 16 P is for Persuasion				
Session 17 Q is for Quarrels				
Session 18 R is for Receiving Compliments				
Session 19 S is for Saying Sorry				
Session 20 T is for Take Turns Talking				
Session 21 U is for Upset				
Session 22 V is for Value				
Session 23 W is for Win/Win				
Session 24 X is for X-ray Eyes				
Session 25 Y is for You				
Session 26 Z is for Zest for Living				

Friendship Log

This Friendship Log belongs to: _____

Name: _____ **Date:** _____

Session: _____

Pair and Share Evaluation

How did we work together today?

Did I:

Face my partner?	Yes/No	☐	☐
Smile and say hello?	Yes/No	☐	☐
Give my partner time to talk?	Yes/No	☐	☐
Listen to my partner?	Yes/No	☐	☐
Finish the conversation politely?	Yes/No	☐	☐

How do you rate yourself in this partnership today?

Excellent	Yes/No	☐	☐
Very good	Yes/No	☐	☐
OK	Yes/No	☐	☐
Help	Yes/No	☐	☐

What might you do differently to make future partnerships go better?

_____

_____

_____

_____

I'm OK

You're OK

Aims

○ To introduce pupils to the programme and its aim which is to teach pupils the skills which will enable them to get along more easily with others and make friends.

○ To introduce pupils to the importance of having a positive attitude to themselves and to others.

Whole Class Introduction

Explain to the class that this is the first session of 'How to make friends'. There are twenty six sessions altogether in the programme. This programme will teach pupils the skills which will help them get along with others and make friends.

It is important to emphasise to the pupils that the skills that we need to get along with others can be learnt. They don't depend on being 'lucky', 'clever' or 'beautiful'. During these sessions pupils will learn how to listen and support others, how to 'read' body talk (body language and facial expressions) and how to behave positively towards others. People who do not manage to learn how to get along with others are often lonely in school and then later when they leave school may find it difficult to get along with their colleagues and keep a job.

Ask pupils to listen to a story which was first told by an American professor called Steve.

I was waiting outside the school gates one day with a teacher watching the parents drop off their children for school. Blustery March winds made it feel even colder than the temperature on the thermometer. The children bundled up against the weather, got out of their cars one after another, said their good-byes and rushed off towards the school. As I continued to watch a blue Honda Accord pulled up and stopped. A mother stepped out the driver-side door and walked round the car and opened the passenger side door for her six year old daughter. The little girl got out, and the two of them stood there looking at each other for a moment. The mother said 'Go make friends now Amy'. She patted her daughter on the head, walked back around the car, opened the car door and drove off. ....Amy looked almost lost in her big coat . Her mother had given her instructions to make friends and Amy was thinking 'Excuse me; how exactly am I going to do that?' (Nowicki, S., 2000, p.144)

Ask the class if they were going to help Amy to make friends what would they tell her?

Encourage the pupils to brainstorm suggestions and scribe their responses on a flip chart. The answer we are looking for in this activity is 'to have a positive attitude' to oneself and others which can be summed up in the phrase.

I'm OK – You're OK

It may be necessary to give pupils a few clues and steer their responses in the right direction so for example if pupils give responses such as 'to like everybody' it is important to pursue this line until pupils arrive at the idea of a positive attitude to self and others. At the end of the brainstorm write on the board:

I'm OK and you're OK

Emphasise to the pupils that it is important to have a positive attitude towards others however before you can have this you need to feel good about yourself. How can you expect someone to like you if you don't like yourself? 'I'm OK' often called self-esteem is a very important part of getting along with others. Someone who has a bad attitude to themselves and others is usually not pleasant to be with and people will probably not want to spend time with that person. It is especially important when meeting people for the first time to think : 'I'm OK and you're OK'. Ask pupils to spend a few minutes discussing these ideas with the person next to them.

Explain to the pupils that thinking 'I'm OK and you're OK' is a very good and healthy way of thinking about all the people we meet and it is what we would like people to think about us when we meet them. Explain to the class that we do our very best thinking when we feel OK about ourselves and the people around us and that positive attitude to ourselves and to others can help us get along together and have fun.

Pair and Share

- Pupils individually complete Activity 1 which involves drawing a picture of themselves looking OK. They can label it if appropriate.

- Pupils then discuss with their partner what it is in their picture that indicates that they are 'OK'.

- Pupils individually complete a 'Pair and Share' evaluation sheet.

Final Plenary

- Ask pupils for any questions or comments on the activity that they have just completed.

- Check that pupils understand the importance of having a positive attitude both to themselves and to others.

- Remind the pupils of the aims of the session and ask them to put their hand up if they consider that out of a score of ten they would give the session five or above for having achieved its aims.

Take Away Activities

- Ask pupils to think about the attitude 'I'm OK, you're OK' others as they watch TV/films/DVDs during the week. Ask the pupils to look carefully for the clues that tell them that people are feeling OK themselves and that they think other people are OK too and use their Friendship Log to record their thoughts.

- Ask pupils to keep a record in their Friendship Log of people that they are in contact with during the week and ask them to think about times that they feel OK and the other people feel OK too.

- Suggest pupils design a poster called 'I'm OK, You're OK'.

A is for Attitude

Draw a picture of yourself looking OK

My name is: _____

Aims

○ To encourage pupils' ability to think flexibly.

○ To teach pupils how to problem solve using a staged approach.

Whole Class Introduction

Explain in this session we are going to think about what to do in some of the problem situations that can arise in school. Reassure pupils that *all* children need to be taught healthy ways of dealing with difficult situations so that they can exert some control on the situation and look after themselves.

Understandably pupils may not want to share difficult experiences openly with the whole class therefore ask pupils to take turns sharing a difficult experience with the person next to them. At the end of this exchange ask the pupils to describe some examples of difficult situations. Emphasise to the pupils that in this activity it is important to talk about behaviours and not name individual pupils.

Previous responses have included:

- When you are called names.

- When people make fun of how you look.

- When people give you a hard time because you got high marks in class.

- When you have a different haircut.

- When your mum collects you from school.

- Nobody talks to you, you are left out.

- Nobody chooses you for their team.

- When you have to read out loud to the class.

The next stage in the discussion is to encourage pupils to explore as a group why some pupils behave in this way. Previous responses have included:

- They want to make themselves look cool.

- They want everybody to be scared of them.

- They don't feel good about themselves

- They might be jealous because they don't get good marks.

- They want to get you into trouble too.

- They want a fight.

- They don't think about how you feel.

Reassure pupils that these sort of difficult behaviours occur in all schools and it is important that in the first instance pupils know there are positive ways of dealing with these situations. Emphasise to the pupils that if they know what to do when they begin to feel that something is wrong then they can begin to sort it out. Explain the following steps with the pupils, reinforcing the positive message that everybody has problems at some point in their lives and knowing how to work out a solution to a problem is an important way of being able to get along with others. Also, emphasise to the pupils that learning how to problem solve is an important way of looking after oneself and also getting along with others.

Explain to the pupils that thinking about traffic lights, red light means stop, amber means wait and green means go, can be a helpful reminder of what to do in a difficult situation.

Stop
First step is to tell yourself to calm down and relax for a moment. Relax and take a deep breath and count to ten. Say something positive to yourself. Tell yourself 'It's going to be OK', 'I will be fine'.

Think
The second step is to think about their choices. What can you do now? Ask pupils for suggestions. These may include:

- Tell an adult.

- Ignore them.

- Walk away.

- Say something friendly to another person and start talking to them.

- Take some very deep breaths.

Think what will be the consequences of doing these things?

Go
The third thing is to decide what is the best thing to do? Decide on something that is helpful but does not hurt others.

Then make the choice and go through with it.

Pair and Share

- Pupils individually complete Activity 2, which involves identifying a problem, and then working through the stages Stop, Wait, Go in order to solve it.

- Pupils then take turns to talk through their work with their partner.

- Pupils individually complete a 'Pair and Share' evaluation sheet.

Final Plenary

- Encourage pupils to reflect upon the session and encourage them to use the steps they have learnt next time they have a problem to solve.

- Suggest to the pupils that as a class they use the steps for problem solving when problem situations arise in school.

- Remind the pupils of the aims of the session and ask them to put their hand up if they consider that out of a score of ten they would give the session five or above for having achieved its aims.

Take Away Activities

- Ask pupils to write or draw about a problem that has happened to them and describe how they solved it in their Friendship Log.

- Ask pupils to look out for examples of people solving problems on television, in films and in books and write about these in their Friendship Log.

- Ask pupils to think about the difficult situations that can occur for individuals while they are reading, watching TV or films and notice the different ways that people deal with them.

STOP
Calm down.
What is the problem?

WAIT
Think about the different things that you could do.

GO
Make a choice and GO!

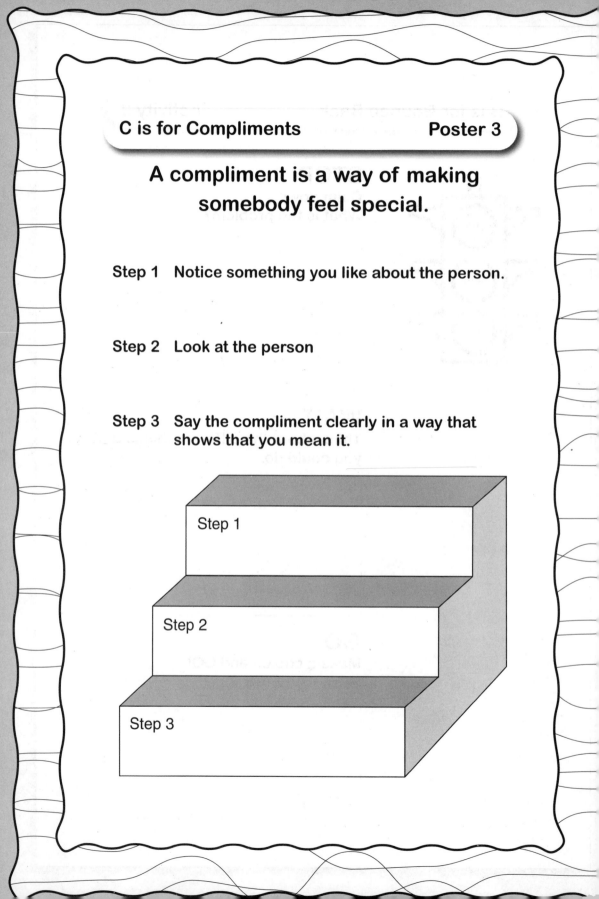

C is for Compliments   **Poster 3**

A compliment is a way of making somebody feel special.

Step 1   Notice something you like about the person.

Step 2   Look at the person

Step 3   Say the compliment clearly in a way that shows that you mean it.

Step 1

Step 2

Step 3

Aims

○ To raise pupils' awareness of specific behaviours that promote getting along with others.

○ To enable pupils to practise how to pay each other compliments so that they receive the affirmation they need to feel fully included in the class and in the school community.

Whole-Class Introduction

Explain to the pupils that this session is going to be about practising one of the most important skills for getting along with others, which is paying compliments.

Paying somebody a compliment means saying something to someone that lets that person know that we appreciate them. Ask pupils to turn to the person next to them and take it in turns to pay each other a compliment. Ask pupils to share some of their compliments.

Summarise for the pupils that there are many different sorts of compliments. A compliment can be about how somebody is behaving and letting them know you have noticed, for example, that they have been kind and thoughtful.

You were very helpful this morning when you found my purse for me.

A compliment can be about celebrating somebody's successes.

That was a really great goal you scored at the end of the game.

A compliment can be about saying positive to somebody about how they look.

You look cool in those new boots.

The important thing to remember about paying compliments is that they must be true.

Explain to the pupils that paying a compliment is often the first step for getting along with others and making friends. Being able to show others that we appreciate them and have noticed something special about them can help us feel comfortable when we are in a situation where we do not know anybody and want to start a conversation. People who know how to pay compliments in a sincere and friendly way have a very good chance of getting along with others. People who say nice things to others usually find out that people are in turn friendly and supportive to them too.

Although paying a compliment is a powerful way of getting along with others sometimes it can be a really difficult thing to do. Ask pupils for their suggestions about why this might be the case.

Emphasise the following two points.

1   Sometimes we don't give compliments because we may feel embarrassed about saying something nice to somebody.

2   Sometimes we may not feel like making somebody feel good because we don't feel always feel good ourselves.

Reassure the pupils that learning the rules for paying a compliment will help them overcome these worries and practising the steps of giving a compliment will make this skill which becomes a natural part of being with others.

If we want to pay somebody a compliment there are four things that can help us.

1. Be a detective
The first step is very important; it is to behave like a detective. Think very carefully about the people around you. Remember these things you may notice about somebody:

•   Something they have done well, their successes.

•   Something good about how the person behaves.

•   Something about how they look; they may have clothes or a hairstyle you like.

2. Choose the right time and right place
Next, think if this is the right time and place to give somebody a compliment? If you are in class and the teacher has asked everybody to keep quiet this will not be a good time to give somebody a compliment.

3. Look at the person
When you are ready to pay somebody a compliment make sure that you look at the person so that they know for sure that you are speaking to them.

4. Say the compliment in a sincere way
The next step is to say the compliment to the person in a way that they will know that you mean it.

Here are the four short rules for paying somebody a compliment:

1 Notice something good about somebody.

2 Right time, right place?

3 Look at the person.

4 Say the compliment so they know you mean it.

Pair and Share

- Pupils individually complete Activity 3, which involves writing different kinds of compliments.

- Pupils then take turns to talk through their work with their partner.

- Pupils individually complete a 'Pair and Share' evaluation sheet.

Final Plenary

- Ask the pupils to reflect upon the session and remind them that most people need a lot of practice in order to develop the habit of noticing good things about others and being able to give sincere compliments.

- Ask pupils to share with the class something that they have learnt during the lesson that they think is important to them.

- At the end of this activity the teacher may wish to emphasise to the class that compliments can make the classroom a warm and friendly place for everyone.

- Remind the pupils of the aims of the session and ask them to put their hand up if they consider that out of a score of ten they would give the session five or above for having achieved its aims.

Take Away Activities

- Pupils record in their Friendship Log the compliments that they receive.

- 3 a Day. Say something nice to three people every day. It is easy to do this if you remember to be a detective always on the look out for good things to say about people. Keep a record of 3 a Day in their Friendship Log.

- Pupils create an A to Z of compliment words in their Friendship Log.

Three ways to compliment people: Make up some compliments for each of the boxes

Friendship Circles

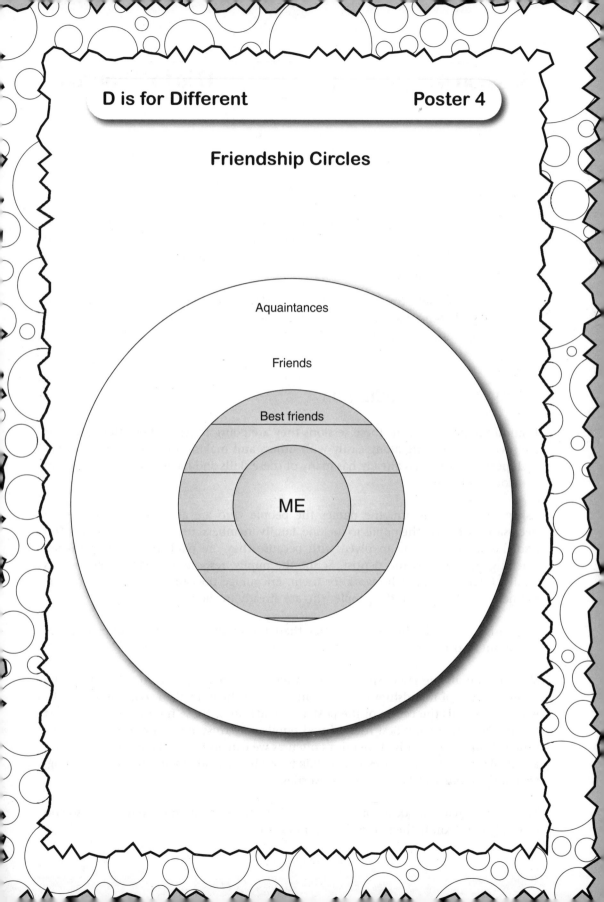

Aims

○ To build on each pupil's self-esteem and encourage them to realise that they all belong and are part of a community. Therefore each member of the class may already have many of the skills that are needed to get along with others and make friends.

○ To raise pupils' awareness of the different kinds of relationships that surround them as individuals and the boundaries that are involved in these different types of relationships.

Whole Class Introduction

Remind the pupils that in these sessions they are going to learn about the skills that are involved in getting along easily with others and making friends. Emphasise that each person in the class already has many of these skills and have shown that they can get along with others.

Ask pupils to brainstorm the names the people who are already in their lives. If necessary encourage the pupils to include, family members, friends, acquaintances and also the adults they are involved with because they are paid to be there, teacher, teaching assistant, doctor, dentist. Scribe the pupils' responses in categories such as family, friends, people who work for them. Encourage the pupils to reflect upon the richness and diversity of the people who are already in their lives.

Emphasise that it is the quality rather than the quantity of relationships that are important in people's lives.

Show the pupils the Friendship Circles Poster 4. Encourage pupils to think about the differing types of friendships that surround each of them. Explain that the first circle, which surrounds the centre of the poster, is made up of those friends who are closest to the pupil. These are 'Best friends' that pupils may trust and share secrets with. We usually want to see our best friends as often as we can and enjoy talking to them a lot about all sorts of things. We especially talk to our best friends about how we are feeling, we tell them our secrets and also our worries.

The second circle is made up of friends that they may see from time to time and so you probably don't know them as well as our best friends.

The third circle is made up of our acquaintances. We might say hello to these people and ask them how they are, we might be in the same team as them and see them at football practice or we might belong to the same club but we don't usually see our acquaintances very often outside that place.

Pair and Share

- Pupils to complete Activity 4. Each pupil completes a friendship circle by using words or drawings and then identifies different sorts of friends by completing sentences.

- Pupils take turns to describe their completed friendship circle with their partner.

- Pupils complete a 'Pair and Share' evaluation.

Final Plenary

- Ask pupils to reflect on their friendship circles and encourage them to feel good about having different sorts of friends.

- Ask the pupils to feedback something important that they have learnt during the session either about themselves or their partner.

Remind the pupils of the aims of the session and ask them to put their hand up if they consider that out of a score of ten they would give the session five or above for having achieved its aims.

Take Away Activities

- Look out for people who are friends in films and on the television and make a list of the friendly behaviours that you see.

- Interview people that you know and ask them about their friendships and how they keep their friends.

- Ask pupils to think about their circle and make a list in their Friendship Log of the skills and qualities, which enable them to make and keep relationships with others.

- Complete a Friendship Circle with a close friend or family member and put this in the Friendship Log.

Fill in the names of people in the different friendship circles.

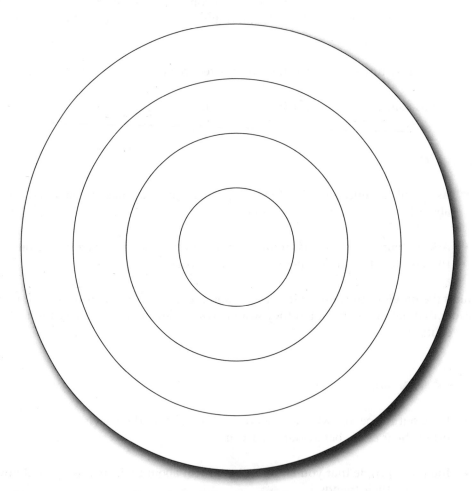

Choose one name for each of the sentences.

_____ is always there for me to talk and play with.

_____ has the same interests as me.

_____ helps me when I'm in trouble.

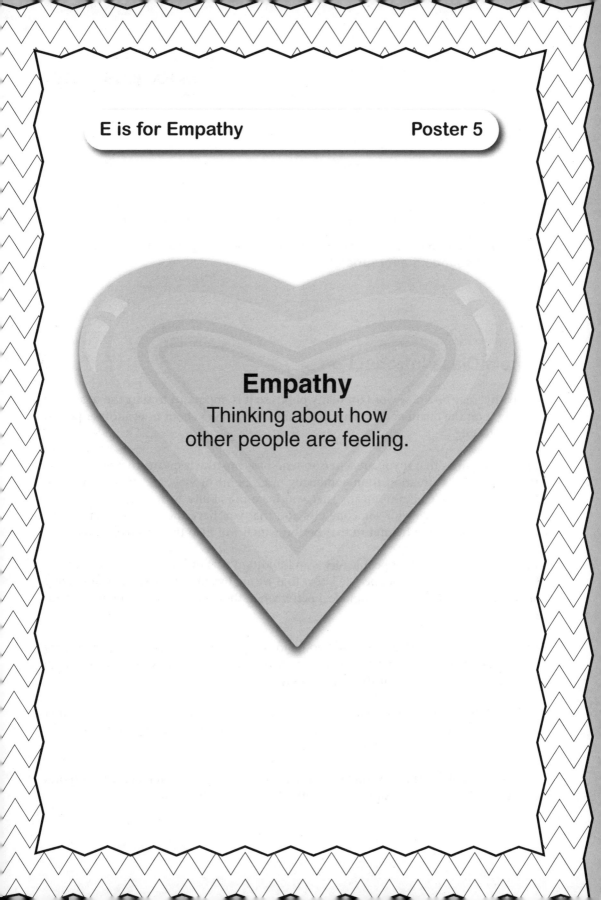

Empathy

Thinking about how
other people are feeling.

Aims

○ To encourage pupils to think about how others may be feeling.

○ To practice using the skills involved in recognising how others are feeling and responding appropriately.

Whole Class Introduction

'Empathy' may be a new word for many pupils so it is important to start the session by writing it on the board and explain that it means thinking about how another person may be feeling.

Explain to pupils that if you are a person who has empathy it means that you are able to think about a situation from somebody else's point of view and treat them with kindness. Having empathy means that you have the ability to recognise a situation which may be difficult for someone else and that you have the understanding to be able to say something helpful to that person which will help them to feel better.

Understanding how other people feel is an important part of getting along with others because it means we can let people know that we are listening to what they are saying and care about them. Most people feel better when they feel that someone is trying to understand how they feel.

Explain to the pupils that there are two main ways in which we can learn about how people are feeling. The first way is to watch people very carefully. The second is to listen very carefully to what they have to say.

Ask pupils to take turns and share with their partner an occasion when they were either able to recognise how somebody was feeling and say something to help them or do something kind that made them feel better.

Ask pupils to share their examples with the class. If pupils are reluctant to respond encourage discussion by using one or both of the examples below.

Example 1

Tom: Is it true you didn't get on the football team again Raj?
Raj: Yes I went to the match but I wasn't chosen again.
Jake: You'll get on the team soon. You are a really good goalie and remember you're much younger than everybody else who was chosen aren't you? You'll get chosen soon and in the meantime you can practice really hard.

Example 2

Ann: Look at that woman's terrible coat?
Jayane: Do you mind, that's my mum you're talking about.
Samira: I think your mum looks great, Jayane. I love vintage and I'm saving up to buy myself a coat just like your mum's. It will take me a long time cos coats like that cost a shed load of money. Not many people can afford them. I think you are lucky because maybe your mum will lend it to you.

Conclude the discussion by emphasising to the pupils that empathy means you care about the feelings of others and you will do your best to protect them from unkind words. If you want kindness for yourself then it is important to give kindness to others.

Pair and Share

Pupils complete Activity 5 which enables them to complete some scenarios:

- Pupils take turns with their partner to discuss the responses.

- Pupils complete a 'Pair and Share' evaluation.

Final Plenary

- Ask pupils to discuss what they have learnt from the session.

- Encourage pupils to think about what they will do differently as a result of the session.

- Remind the pupils of the aims of the session and ask them to put their hand up if they consider that out of a score of ten they would give the session five or above for having achieved its aims.

Take Away Activities

- Write a short story or poem in your Friendship Log about a time when somebody said something to you to make you feel better after your feelings had been hurt.

- While watching TV or DVD look out for examples of people who help other people feel better after they have been upset. Record your examples in your Friendship Log.

- Record the times in your Friendship Log when you notice how other people are feeling.

Your friend forgot his packed lunch. You have a large packed lunch. What could you say to your friend?

_____

_____

_____

_____

Your friend is very upset because she has lost her cat. She has been looking everywhere for the cat. What could you say to your friend?

_____

_____

_____

_____

It's your friend's birthday and you know her mother is in hospital so she won't have a party. What could you say to your friend?

_____

_____

_____

_____

One of your friends is very worried because she has to go to the doctors for an injection before she goes on holiday. What could you say to your friend?

_____

_____

_____

_____

Fair

UnFair

Aims

○ To encourage pupils to think about fair and unfair behaviours.

○ To enable pupils to think of various ways of acting fairly in their dealings with others·

Whole Class Introduction

Open the session by telling the class that you (the teacher) need a new pen, (or pencil case, lunch box – choose an item of equipment that obviously is a personal possession of a pupil and is readily available in the classroom).

Illustrative script

'I need a new pen, here's a new pen that looks as though it will not run out for a long time, I'm going to have it because I need a new pen to write a letter.'

Ask the class if I took that pen would I be behaving in a fair way?

Encourage the pupils to discuss whether the teacher would be fair in taking something that belonged to somebody else because she needed it to do her work?

Summarise and scribe the main points of the pupils' discussion. Explain that being fair in the way we treat people is an important way of getting along with others. Emphasise to the class that if we do things that are clearly not fair we will upset people and they will not want to spend time with us. Making sure that we behave fairly is an important way of getting along with others although it isn't always easy and sometimes it can be tempting to think about what we need and not think about the other person.

Ask the pupils for examples of fair and unfair behaviour. Remind the pupils to describe behaviours and not include the names of pupils in their examples. Scribe their contributions.

Ask the pupils to take turns with the pupil next to them to share an example of a time when they consider that they were treated unfairly. Ask the pupils to discuss with their partner how the situation made them feel and whether they were happy with the way they behaved. Ask pupils to work out a different solution that would have made everybody involved feel OK. Ask for pupils who are prepared to share their discussions with the whole class.

End the discussion by asking the pupils to suggest some of the things that they can do make sure that they are fair in their dealings with others.

Previous responses have included:

- Sharing and taking turns to use books, equipment.

- Helping to clear up at the end of a game or activity.

- Putting clothes and belongings away and being responsible for your own area.

Tell the pupils that in order to sort out if a solution was a good one they can ask themselves the following three questions:

1. Was it a safe thing to do?

2. Was it an honest thing to do?

3. How did I feel at the end?

Tell the pupils that if the solution we choose to deal with a difficult situation is safe, if it is honest and if it leaves everybody involved feeling fine then it has been a fair way of dealing with things.

Pair and Share

Ask the pupils to complete Activity 6, which asks them to decide if certain behaviours are fair or unfair.

- Pupils take turns with their partner to discuss the responses.

- Pupils complete a 'Pair and Share' evaluation.

Final Plenary

- Ask the pupils whether using the three questions they have learnt today were helpful in sorting out problems fairly.

- Ask the pupils what they will do differently as a result of the session.

- Remind the pupils of the aims of the session and ask them to put their hand up if they consider that out of a score of ten they would give the session five or above for having achieved its aims.

Take Away Activities

- Keep a record in the Friendship Log of the times when pupils come across an unfair situation and describe how the situation was sorted out.

- Make a record in the Friendship Log of unfair situations from the TV, DVDs, books and newspapers and if possible include how they were resolved.

Fair or Unfair	Fair	Unfair
Dropping litter.	☐	☐
One of your friends shares chocolate with the class but leaves you out.	☐	☐
You miss your train by one minute.	☐	☐
Making a lot of noise.	☐	☐
Not helping in the house.	☐	☐
Your friend gets much more pocket money than you.	☐	☐
Your dad always watches sport on TV so you can't see your favourite programme.	☐	☐
You are one minute late for the bus and you miss it.	☐	☐
Your mum won't let you have a dog.	☐	☐

Get over it

Understand the other person's point of view

Don't hurt the other person back

Give the other person a chance

Aims

○ To raise pupils' awareness of the importance of being able to forgive others.

○ To enable pupils to explore their feelings around forgiveness.

Whole Class Introduction

Begin the session by encouraging the pupils to think about the last time they were angry with somebody and ask them to describe how they felt.

Reassure pupils that falling out with friends or having disagreements with others can make us very angry or very sad and if our feelings continue then we may hold a grudge or bad feelings against them.

Alex was very upset because her best friend Samira had a spare ticket for a concert and chose another friend to go with her . Alex felt very angry and very left out. What's the point of being her best friend she thought if she chooses somebody else to give her spare ticket to. I always choose Samira first for everything, I hang around waiting for her when we go out she's always late and keeps me waiting and then she leaves me out and chooses Keira over me. Alex was very angry she did not want to see or speak to Samira again. Alex walked home from school alone and went straight up to her room to do her homework. Later that evening Samira called around to see her. Samira said to her, 'Look I know you don't want to see me but I have come to say sorry to you about the concert I should have asked you but that was Keira's favourite band and I didn't think you would want to go.' Alex still felt very angry with Samira 'I hate you for taking Keira to the concert with you instead of me. I wouldn't do that to you. You were so out of order doing that.' Samira said, 'Look, I'm so sorry I know I should have talked to you about it first. I am really really sorry. Please forgive me.' Alex did not feel like forgiving Samir,a she felt like never speaking to her again. She was still very angry and very hurt. Samira could tell how angry Alex was and decided there was no point in hanging about and started to walk away. Alex watched her friend walk down the street Samira had her head down and she was walking very slowly. She looked very upset. Alex did not like seeing her friend look so upset and shouted after her, 'Hey wait, Samira. Look it's OK, I forgive you but next time will you talk to me about what is happening. You're my best friend.'

Getting over angry and hurt feelings can be a very difficult thing for us to do. We can still feel that the person is in the wrong but at the same time we don't want to hurt them and we still value their friendship and we don't want to lose them as a friend.

Sometimes it helps not to see the person when we are angry with them so that we give ourselves time to cool down before we talk to them again.

When we forgive somebody we have to separate the person from their behaviour. We can say to them 'Look I don't like what you did to me but I still want you to be my friend'. Forgiving somebody means you want to understand how the other person feels and give the friendship another chance. The most important thing about forgiveness is that we don't hurt the other person back that we are willing to forget about the hurt or angry feelings they have caused us and we give the friendship another chance.

Ask pupils to think about how it feels to be forgiven.

Forgiving means that even though you may still feel angry and hurt you can get over your anger and see things from the other person's point of view. Instead of getting into a fight and hurting them back, getting over it means that you tell the person you really want to give the friendship another go.

Getting over angry feelings can feel good. If we don't get over them we can get stuck with our our angry and hurt feelings and waste time feeling miserable when we could be having fun.

Remind the pupils of the rules for helping themselves get over angry or upset feelings

- Understand the other person's point of view.

- Don't hurt the other person back.

- Give the other person a chance.

Pair and Share

Ask the pupils to work in pairs to complete Activity 7 which asks them to identify times when they were cross or upset but got over it.

- Pupils take turns with their partner to discuss the responses.

- Pupils complete a 'Pair and Share' evaluation.

Final Plenary

- Pupils share with the class something new that they learnt today about getting over angry or hurt feelings.

- Encourage pupils to think about how they would like to act next time that somebody says 'sorry' to them.

- Remind the pupils of the aims of the session and ask them to put their hand up if they consider that out of a score of ten they would give the session five or above for having achieved its aims.

Take Away Activities

Keep a record in the Friendship Log of the times when pupils come across a situation where somebody is angry with somebody else but were able to get over their angry feelings and forgive them.

Make a record in the Friendship Log of situations from TV, DVDs, books and newspapers where people are angry with each other and, if possible, include how they were resolved.

In your Friendship Log write a story or draw a picture with the title 'Don't let the sun go down on your anger'.

These are the times when even though I was cross or upset, I said OK and got over it.

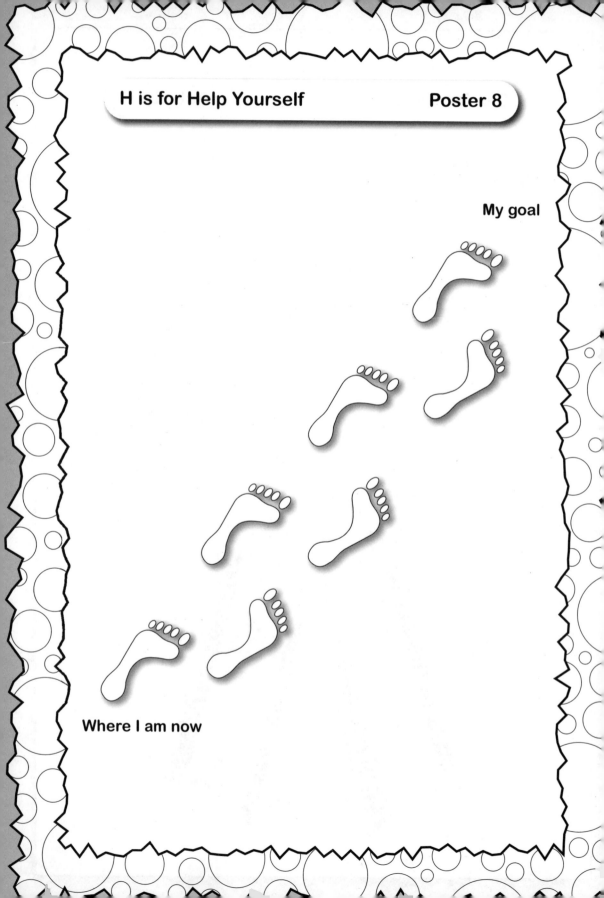

Aims

○ To introduce pupils to the concept of helping them selves by identifying goals.

○ To encourage the pupils to identify individual goals for themselves in order to develop their friendship skills.

Whole Class Introduction

Explain to the pupils that in order to get better at getting along with people and making friends it is important to have a healthy lifestyle and identify goals that they can achieve in order to enable themselves to feel better. Ask pupils for examples of the goals that they would like to achieve in order to improve their ability to get along with others.

Previous responses have included:

- Get fit so I can play sports better.

- Lose weight so I look better.

- Improve football skills.

- Learn to dance.

- Learn to sing.

- Learn how to play chess and join chess club.

Explain to the pupils that improving our life and getting better at things does not happen overnight. It is important to understand that reaching our goals is like a journey made up of lots and lots of very small steps. Knowing that we are moving towards reaching our goal through these small steps will help us to feel a lot better about ourselves.

Ask the pupils to choose from the responses above and suggest some of the small steps that they could make towards achieving a goal. Emphasise to the pupils that this process does not mean that there is a right or wrong way of doing things but that there is a way of behaving or making choices that can lead to very positive outcomes and help us to feel good about ourselves.

Ask pupils to take turns and share with the person next to them some suggestions of what small steps they could take towards a goal which is important for them.

Ask pupils to share some of the important issues that have come out of their discussions.

Emphasise to the pupils that when we want to get fit or change the way our body looks, it doesn't happen overnight. A body builder doesn't expect to have the perfect muscles a few days after starting to go to the gym. The best way to get ourselves to help ourselves is to have a goal by taking small positive steps towards the goal.

Ask each of the pupils to decide on a goal and then decide on a scale of 1–10 where they are now in terms of being close to getting their goal. Ask the pupils where would they like to be on the scale? Next the pupils need to identify the steps they need to take in order to arrive at their goal.

Pair and Share

Pupils complete Activity 8 which asks them to identify and consider where they are now and how they will move forward to the goal.

- Pupils take turns with their partner to discuss the responses.

- Pupils complete a 'Pair and Share' evaluation.

Final Plenary

- Ask pupils to share something new they learnt from the session.

- Ask pupils what they will do differently as a result of the session.

- Remind the pupils of the aims of the session and ask them to put their hand up if they consider that out of a score of ten they would give the session five or above for having achieved its aims.

Take Away Activities

- Pupils make a list of the things that they can do to make sure they have a healthy lifestyle in their Friendship Log.

- Ask the pupils to make a chart on which they can record the small steps that they make towards achieving their goal.

- Ask pupils to watch TV or look in newspapers or magazines for examples of people who have achieved their goals. These can be singers, athletes or anybody who has achieved an important goal.

- Write a story or draw a picture with the title 'Going for Gold'.

H is for Help Yourself   Activity 8

Name:_____   Date:_____

My goal is:_____

_____

Where are you now? Circle the number:

1   2   3   4   5   6   7   8   9   10

Why am I at number_____?

I would like to be at number_____.

Write about the small steps that you will have to take to get there.

_____

_____

_____

_____

Invitation

You are invited to a Fancy Dress Party at my house. It will start at 4.30p.m. and finish at 6.30p.m. on Saturday 14th March. I do hope that you can come.

24 Church Road
Anytown

RSVP

Aims

○ **To enable pupils to understand that invitations are an important part of friendship.**

○ **To encourage pupils to explore different sorts of invitations.**

Whole Class Introduction

Explain to the class that invitations are very important. They are a way of letting people know that you like them and want to spend time with them.

If pupils have already completed Session 4 'D is for Different' ask pupils to refer back to their relationship circle and think about which people in their circle they have given an invitation to and where did they invite them to? Scribe their responses.

Emphasise to the pupils that inviting somebody to do something with you is a way of making that person feel special and if they say 'Yes' means that you will be able to spend time with that person and get to know them. If you ask somebody to visit you at your house it is important that you get permission first from your mum or dad and then the person you are inviting must get permission from their mum or dad too.

When you invite somebody to your house it is important that you have some activities to do that the other person will enjoy. You don't want the person to be bored in your house. Also ask your mum if you can have a snack to share with your friend. When you invite somebody to do something with you, to visit your house or go to the shops remember to ask them when they are alone and remember to smile at the person, make eye contact and ask them in a clear, kind voice. Giving one person an invitation and leaving other people out can make those people feel left out and miserable.

Ask pupils to talk to their partner about giving an invitation then brainstorm the different sorts of invitations that they can make? Previous responses have included.

- Sleep overs.

- Birthday party.

- Barbeque.

- Christmas party.

- Christening.

- Cinema.

Pair and Share

Pupils complete Activity 9 which asks them to either design or write an invitation to a party.

- Pupils take turns with their partner to discuss the responses.

- Pupils complete a 'Pair and Share' evaluation.

Final Plenary

- Ask pupils to reflect on what they have learnt in the session.

- Ask the pupils to remember the important rules to use when they are making an invitation.

- Remind the pupils of the aims of the session and ask them to put their hand up if they consider that out of a score of ten they would give the session five or above for having achieved its aims.

Take Away Activities

- Practice going out of your way to invite pupils who look lonely in school to join in with your group or go up and talk to them if they are alone.

- Watch out for examples of people inviting other to do things with them on TV and in films. Write about these examples in the Friendship Log.

- In your Friendship Log make a list of the invitations you receive and the invitations you give to others.

Date:_____

Design an invitation for a guest that you would like to invite to a party. You can choose to make a card or write a letter.

Session 10

J is for Joining In

Aims

○ To provide pupils with a practical strategy for joining in activities and conversations with their peers.

○ To enable pupils to practice the skills of joining in

Whole Class Introduction

Explain to the class that in this session we are going to learn about how to join in and play with others who are already playing a game or join a group who are already busy with an activity.

Ask the pupils why they think it is important to learn how to join in with others. Scribe pupils' responses.

Previous responses have included:

• It will help us get to know each other.

• It is fun to play with a group.

• It is lonely to look at others playing and not be able to join in.

• We might be very interested in what they are doing and want to have a go.

• Trying to join in a game is very scary.

Summarise from the pupil discussion that joining in is an important skill to learn because it can create lots of opportunities to get to know others and have fun.

We all seem to all agree that sometimes we will all want to join in with others while they are playing a game or doing an interesting activity. Sometimes it can be difficult to join in however because the others are so busy playing their game or doing their activity that it is hard to get them to listen to us. You have to wait for just the right moment to ask to join in especially if the game has already started. If we do it the wrong way we probably won't get to join in the game.

Rules for Joining In

- The first thing to remember is to look at the person we want to speak to and make eye contact and smile.

- Next step is to say Hi.

- Then it is important to *wait* for the right time to speak.

Waiting is very important. It is just like waiting for the right time to cross the road. If the group is very busy or at an exciting point in the game they will not be ready to listen. Only when the time is right, ask if you can join in.

Ask pupils to take turns sharing with the pupil next to them their experiences of joining in. Then ask pupils to share experiences with the whole group. Pupils often report that they have found joining in a very difficult thing to do so it is important to end this part of the session with some helpful suggestions that the pupils can use. These include:

- Before you start to join a group think about whether the group looks friendly. Only decide to join the group if you think it looks friendly.

- Choose to join a group only if they are doing the things which you enjoy doing. If the group is playing a game you don't like don't even think about joining in.

- If you join a group do not start to change things straight away, fit in with what the others are doing and play the game their way.

- Think about how many people are in the group. It is easiest to join in a group if there are more than four people in the group. It is most difficult to join a group if there are only two other people in the group.

- No is not the same as never. If you ask to join in a group and they say 'No' do not be put off and ask again another day. Always remember 'No' can mean 'next time'.

Pair and Share

Ask pupils to complete Activity 10 in pairs which provides various scenarios and asks if the situation is one in which they should ask to join in.

- Pupils take turns with their partner to discuss the responses.

- Pupils complete a 'Pair and Share' evaluation.

Final Plenary

- Relax and remember: what are the important things they will remember from the session.

- Ask the pupils to think about the session and suggest what they will put into practice straightaway.

- Remind the pupils of the aims of the session and ask them to put their hand up if they consider that out of a score of ten they would give the session five or above for having achieved its aims.

Take Away Activities

- Ask pupils to keep a record in the Friendship Log of the times when they practice joining a group or a game and to include what they do to make sure they are successful and able to join a game or activity.

- Keep a record of the times when other pupils ask to join their game and notice how they do it in the Friendship Log.

Date:_____

Would you ask to join in?   Yes ☐   No ☐

You see two friends having a quiet talk together in the corner of the playground.   ☐   ☐

A large group of boys and girls are playing together in the playground.   ☐   ☐

A group of your friends are going to the library after lunch.   ☐   ☐

Two of your friends are doing a special project together.   ☐   ☐

Think of you own examples.

_____

_____

_____

_____

Trust

Truth

Doing

K is for Keep Your Word

Aims

○ To introduce pupils to the importance of being keeping your word and being trustworthy as an important part of getting along with others.

○ To practice ways of improving 'Keeping your word'.

Whole Class Introduction

Explain to the pupils that keeping your word means being trustworthy and that this is an important part of getting along with others.

Ask pupils to think about what 'keeping your word' and being trustworthy means to them and to illustrate it with examples from their own lives.

(If the class has already covered Session 4 'D is for Different' it may be helpful for pupils to use their Friendship Circle as a prompt for this discussion.)

It is likely that during this discussion pupils may refer more to the adults in their lives than their peers. It is helpful to encourage pupils to reflect on this and emphasise that as they get older 'Keeping your word' and being trustworthy becomes more and more important.

Ask pupils to give examples of times when a friend or acquaintance has not kept their word and describe how it made them feel. Remind pupils that it is important not to use names during this discussion but to talk about behaviours and feelings.

Previous examples have included:

- Not turning up.

- Cancelling arrangements at the last moment without a good reason.

- Not keeping a secret.

- Talking about me behind my back.

- Promising to help but then not keeping your word.

- Being a good friend one day but not the next.

- Talking about my other friends.

- Telling me lies.

- Cheating.

Explain to the pupils that keeping your word really means treating your others like you would want to be treated yourself. If you let other people down you may not feel good about yourself because you know that you are doing something that is unkind. Most people choose to spend their time with people who keep their word.

Discuss with the class the following points:

- We like to spend time with people we can trust.

- We want to know that people are telling us the truth.

- We want to be able to trust people to do what they say they will do.

Pair and Share

Pupils complete Activity 11 which asks them to identify people they trust to keep their word.

- Pupils take turns with their partner to discuss the responses.

- Pupils complete a 'Pair and Share' evaluation.

Final Plenary

- Relax and remember: encourage pupils to discuss what are the important things they will remember from the session.

- Ask the pupils to think about the importance of 'keeping their word' and suggest what they will be able to put into practice straightaway.

- Remind the pupils of the aims of the session and ask them to put their hand up if they consider that out of a score of ten they would give the session five or above for having achieved its aims.

Take Away Activities

- Ask pupils to keep a record in the Friendship Log of the times when they 'keep their word with friends and family.

- Keep a record of the times when other people keep their word and how it feels.

- Write a story or draw a picture called 'Keeping my word'.

K is for Keep Your Word

Date:_____

My Stars

Think of three people you trust to keep their word!

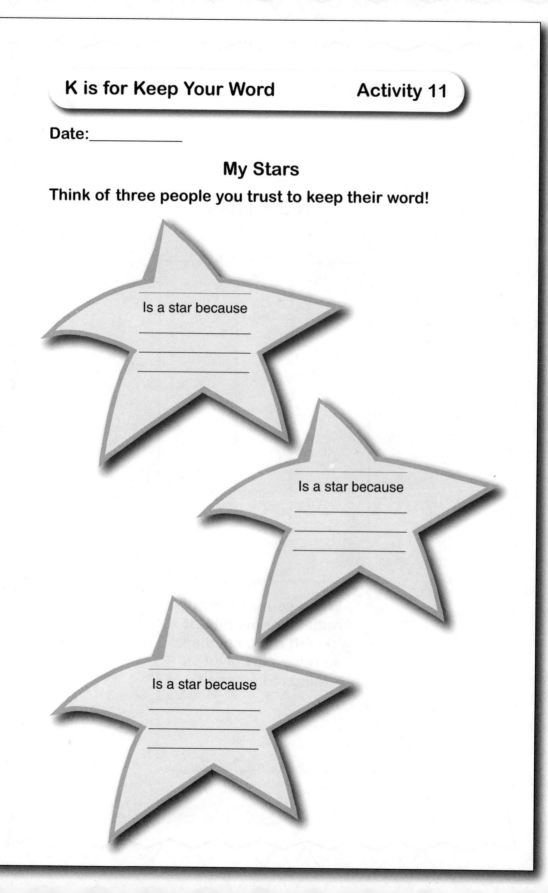

Is a star because
_____
_____
_____

Is a star because
_____
_____
_____

Is a star because
_____
_____
_____

No Entry

When you get left out remember everybody gets left out sometimes so relax. Say positive things to yourself.

Aims

○ To encourage pupils to use positive self talk.

○ To enable pupils to manage being left out.

Whole Class Introduction

In this session we are going to be thinking about how to manage a difficult situation that happens to all of us from time to time – being left out.

Ask pupils to describe what being 'left out' means to them.

Previous responses have included:

- No one to talk to.

- Everybody else is talking and laughing but not to me.

- Everybody else knows each other really well.

- I don't fit in.

- I'm not good at games so I don't fit in with my class.

Now we are going to listen to a story. This story is about a famous British artist called Tracey.

Tracey lives alone in a big house in London with her cat called Docket. Tracey does sewing and drawing and painting and you can see lots of her work in a big art gallery in London which is called the Tate Modern. When Tracey was a little girl she lived by the sea with her mum and her twin brother Paul. When Tracey was seven years old she said to her mum 'One of the girls in my class, it's her birthday and this evening she's having a party. Can I go? After school Tracey put on her favourite party dress. Her Mum carefully wrapped some jewellery in tissue paper for a gift and then Tracey walked up the road. Outside school, five or six girls stood around in lovely princess dresses. The birthday girl arrived with her dad in a big, shiny, white limousine, and as everybody went to get in the limousine the birthday girl said to Tracey 'You can't come to the party'. The birthday girl's father said to Tracey 'I'm afraid you're not invited. You don't have an invitation'. The limousine drove away without Tracey, Tracey waited outside school for as long as she could, then she hid the jewellery and went home. Her Mum said 'Did you have a lovely time at the party? Tracey said 'Yes' it was lovely. That night Tracey cried herself to sleep. She cried and cried. In the morning she said: 'Mummy what's an invitation?'

Ask pupils for their responses to this story? Ask pupils to think about at what point in the story could things have been sorted out so Tracey did not get upset?

Ask the class to spend a few moments sharing with a partner about their own experience of being left out.

Encourage the pupils to begin to think about why pupils might leave others out.

Previous responses have included:

- They might not realise that anybody is left out.

- They are only thinking about themselves because they are having fun talking to each other and are not thinking about anybody else.

- They don't mean to leave you out they are just not thinking.

- They don't know you feel left out.

- They think they belong to a gang and nobody else can join in.

Emphasise to pupils that they can do something about feeling left out and that they can make themselves feel better. Work through the following stages with the class ensuring that they understand each step of the process. When they realise that they are being left out:

- Calm down and relax. Take deep breaths.

- Think about what is happening and how you feel.

- Think about what you could you do to make yourself feel better.

Responses to this have included:

- Move straightaway and find something more interesting to do.

- Just stay there and look like you belong.

- Wait for a good moment to say something and join in.

- Stay there until the right moment comes for you to move quickly away.

Choose the best solution

It is important to emphasise to the pupils that choosing the best solution doesn't mean that there is just one right thing to do. Choosing the best solution means that what you do depends on how you feel and on the situation. If you feel very upset or angry at being left out it the best thing may be to walk away. If you feel you would really like to join in then waiting for the right moment to say something maybe the best thing to do.

Ask pupils to discuss what Tracey could have done differently in the story?

Pair and Share

Pupils complete Activity 12 which asks pupils to decide on a range of responses to being left out.

- Pupils take turns with their partner to discuss the responses.

- Pupils complete a 'Pair and Share' evaluation.

Final Plenary

- Encourage pupils to reflect on what they have learnt during the session.

- Emphasise to the pupils that although 'Being Left Out' is usually not a good feeling it is important that they 'get a grip', remain calm and think positively about the situation. Emphasise to the pupils that everybody gets left out from time to time.

- Remind the pupils of the aims of the session and ask them to put their hand up if they consider that out of a score of ten they would give the session five or above for having achieved its aims.

Take Away Activities

- Encourage pupils to notice times during the coming week when they feel left out and think about how they deal with the situation. Record their thoughts in the Friendship Log.

- Watch TV or films and think about times when people may feel left out. Write about this in the Friendship Log.

- Encourage pupils to notice if any of their classmates look lonely or left out in school especially in the playground and make a special effort to include them in the group or to start a conversation with them.

- Write a story or draw a picture called 'Left out'.

Date:_____

If I'm left out I can think:

Other things I can say, think or do.

_____

_____

_____

_____

_____

_____

The Ripple Effect

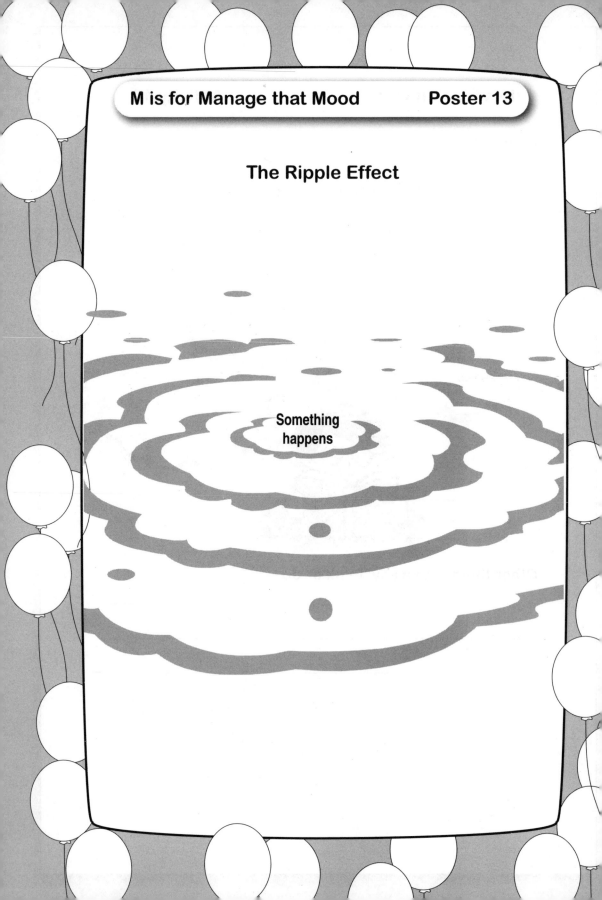

Something
happens

M is for Manage that Mood

Aims

○ To enable pupils to identify their feelings when things go wrong.

○ To teach pupils to understand how to let go of uncomfortable feelings and manage bad moods.

Whole Class Introduction

Begin the lesson by asking pupils to think about a time when they were in a very bad mood. Reassure pupils that everybody gets in a bad mood from time to time and so being in a bad mood is not something that they have to be ashamed or feel bad about.

Ask pupils to share briefly with person next to them a bad mood experience.

Ask the pupils to think about why they got into that bad mood and whether, when they were in that bad mood, they were unfriendly or unkind to somebody they knew? Again reassure pupils that this is nothing to be ashamed of and the important thing is to understand that if we have a quarrel or an upset with somebody the uncomfortable feelings can stay with us for a long time and can spill over into other activities. Explain to the pupils that being in a bad mood can be like a pebble being thrown into a pool of water. Lots of ripples or water come out from where the pebble hit the water. Explain to the pupils that it is important to learn to manage our bad moods so that they do not spread out like the ripples of water and do damage to other parts of our life.

Think about the following story:

Tina was finishing a story on her computer for her English homework. Tina had been working for two weeks on this story and she was really enjoying doing it because her mother had bought her a voice-activated programme which meant that Tina didn't have to think about spellings she could just speak to the computer and concentrate on making up a really exciting adventure. Suddenly towards the end of the story Tina said 'Stop, get rid of it all'. Suddenly Tina noticed that the screen had gone blank the story had disappeared. Tina realised what she had done. She was very frustrated that the computer didn't know that when she said 'Stop, get rid of it all' Tina was thinking about words to add to her adventure story instead the computer had deleted the story which had taken her two weeks to complete. Tina was very worried she didn't know what she was going to tell her teacher. Then Tina became very angry that the homework that had taken her two weeks to do was gone. The next day Tina got up late and went to school in a terrible mood. The first lesson was English. When she walked into the class her friend Tracey said 'Hi, Tina, you look fed up, what's wrong? Tina snapped 'Oh go away, just leave me alone'.

Ask the class to think about the following questions:

- What was Tina's problem?

- How did she first feel about that problem?

- Why did Tina tell Tracey to go away?

Explain to the class that in the story Tina had started with a problem which made her feel frustrated and worried and then she had grown angry and got into a bad mood which she had taken out on her friend Tracey.

Ask pupils to suggest what Tina could have done differently. Scribe their suggestions.

Discuss with the pupils the following guidelines for managing bad moods.

- First step is to recognise you are in a bad mood.

- Secondly take some time to do things which are going to make you feel better.

- Thirdly understand that it takes time for feelings to go away.

Ask class to brainstorm some of the things that they could do to make themselves feel better.

Previous responses have included:

- Phone a friend.

- Kick a football hard

- Listen to very loud music.

- Go swimming.

- Work on your favourite hobby.

- Tidy your bedroom and throw all the old rubbish out.

- Go for a long run or walk.

Pair and Share

Ask pupils to complete Activity 13 which asks the pupils to identify and draw getting in and out of moods.

- Pupils take turns with their partner to discuss the responses.

- Pupils complete a 'Pair and Share' evaluation.

Final Plenary

- Ask pupils to feedback on the work they have been doing in pairs.

- Ask them what they will do differently next time they are in a bad mood as a result of the session.

- Remind the pupils of the aims of the session and ask them to put their hand up if they consider that out of a score of ten they would give the session five or above for having achieved its aims.

Take Away Activities

- In the Friendship Logs make a list of the things pupils can do help themselves manage a bad mood. Suggest that if pupils have a particular problem with bad moods they should copy their three favourite ways of managing bad moods on a postcard and carry the card with them and use it as a reminder of what to do next time they get into a bad mood.

- Watch TV or films and write in the Friendship Log about the sorts of things that put people in bad moods and what they do about them.

- In your Friendship Log write a letter to Amir who wants advice on what to do about his bad moods?

'When I get home from school I am usually in such a bad mood. My head is banging and I feel like I want to shout. I can't concentrate on doing my homework so when I get back to school again the next day I am in trouble all over again? Please help me. What can I do about my bad moods?'

M is for Manage that Mood   Activity 13

Date:_____

Write and draw about your moods.

This is the thing that puts me in a mood. _____

_____

_____

_____

_____

These are the things that I can do to help myself to feel better. ——

_____

_____

_____

_____

_____

Next time I'm in a bad mood I'll try:

_____

_____

_____

_____

_____

_____

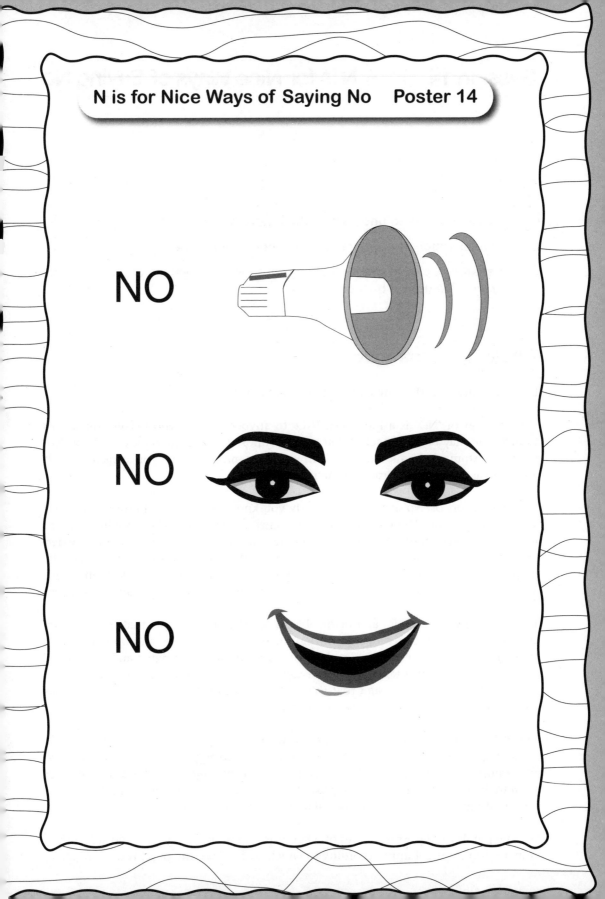

Aims

○ To enable pupils to understand the different sorts of 'No'.

○ To enable pupils to understand the importance of being able to say 'No'.

○ To enable pupils to practice standing up for themselves and saying 'No' in ways that do not hurt others.

Whole Class Introduction

Explain to the class that there are different sorts of 'No'.

The first sort of 'NO' is a loud clear 'NO' to anybody at all who makes you feel as though you may be in danger. If you are uncomfortable it is important to shout 'No' from your stomach. Shout like a foghorn not like a mouse so that you attract as much attention as possible and scare off the person.

The second sort of 'No' is when somebody you know asks you to do something that you know is wrong. There are times when someone may ask you to shoplift or cheat during a test. Remember that you have the right to say 'No' and there are times when you should say 'No'. It helps if you think about what to do in advance. Say 'No' clearly, keep your head firmly on the ground and your head and shoulders held high. Don't smile and keep good eye contact. Then the other person will know you mean business.

Knowing when to say 'No' and being able to tell the other people that the way that they are behaving is unreasonable without being rude to them is an important thing to learn. Being able to say 'No' is about standing up for your rights and not letting other people take advantage of you. Reassure the class that most people have to learn how and when to say 'No' and that this is especially important when somebody asks us to do something that we know we should not do.

The third sort of no is when somebody who we know and like wants us to do something we don't feel like doing. There is nothing wrong with the person asking us for example to go shopping with them or to go swimming it just happens we don't want to do it so it is important to say 'No' kindly but as though we mean it. It can often be very difficult to say 'No' because we don't want to hurt the person's feelings.

Ask the pupils to suggest examples of when it is important to say 'No' and scribe their responses in three columns according to which sort of 'No' the pupil is describing.

Explain to the pupils that there are some rules which can help them say 'No' firmly. First of all it is important to stay calm, taking a deep breath can help. Secondly it is important to look at the person. Thirdly it is important to use 'I' talk. This means to start with the word 'I'. Examples of using 'I' talk include:

Thank you for inviting me to go to your party but I am really sorry I won't be able to come because I will be on holiday. I hope I will be able to see you when I get back.

Thanks for asking me to go swimming with you but I am going to see my dad. I hope we can go swimming another day.

Thanks for asking me to go to see that film but I really don't feel like seeing that film. I would like to go and see another film with you one day.

Pair and Share

Pupils to complete Activity 14 which asks the pupils how they would respond in a variety of situations.

- Pupils take turns with their partner to discuss the responses.

- Pupils complete a 'Pair and Share' evaluation.

Final Plenary

- Encourage pupils to remember what they have learnt in the session about saying no.

- Ask pupils to think about what they will do differently as a result of the session.

- Remind the pupils of the aims of the session and ask them to put their hand up if they consider that out of a score of ten they would give the session five or above for having achieved its aims.

Take Away Activities

- Look for examples of people using different sorts of 'No' on TV and in films etc. Write about these in your Friendship Log.

- Make a list of all the times that you say 'No' to people. Remember to describe the different sorts of 'No' that you use.

- Design a 'Just Say No' poster.

N is for Nice Ways of Saying No   Activity 14

Date: _____

Write or draw answers to these situations.

Your friend telephones you and wants you to come over to her house. You have already promised to visit another friend.

_____

_____

_____

Your friend sits next to you in a test and wants to copy your answers.

_____

_____

_____

Your friends asks if he can bring another person to your birthday arty but you don't like that person.

_____

_____

_____

Make up some of your own examples.

_____

_____

_____

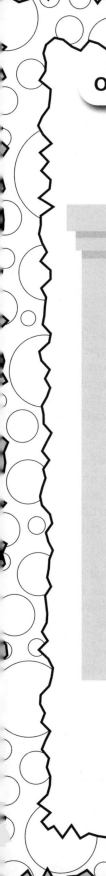

Special offers

Relax

Smiles

Hi's

Aims

○ To raise pupils' awareness of how to open a conversation.

○ To enable pupils to practise the skills involved in opening conversations.

Whole Class Introduction

Explain to the pupils that if they want to get along well with others and make friends, one of the most important things that they need to learn to is how to open up a conversation. This is an important skill that they will need in lots of different places. When pupils go into a new class or start at a new school they may find it very difficult to approach other people. They may feel shy or embarrassed and although they may want to go up to somebody and speak to them they can get very scared because they think they will not know what to say to the other person.

If we don't know a person it can be very difficult to start talking to them because we don't know what questions to ask them and we may feel scared that they may not want to talk to us. Ask pupils to remember the last time they felt nervous about starting a conversation with somebody and to spend two minutes sharing this experience with the person next to them. Ask pupils to take it in turns to talk and remind the class after a minute that it is time for the other person to speak.

After pupils have had the opportunity to share their experiences explain that in this lesson we are going to learn some rules which will help us open conversations. First of all we are going to learn how to calm down and feel positive about ourselves and secondly we are going to learn what to say to somebody who we don't know.

First of all when we notice somebody we would like to talk to but don't know what to say the important thing is to chill. Calm down and say something positive to ourselves. Sometimes when we see somebody we would like to talk to we can get into a panic and all we can think is 'What shall I say?'. Ask the class for examples of positive things that they could say to themselves to help them calm down. Scribe the responses as it is important to enable the class to build up a rich variety of positive comments that they can say to themselves in difficult situations.

The second step is to go straight ahead, smile, say 'hi' to the person and tell them your name.

The smile is probably the most important part of this second step. If somebody says hello to us with a miserable or angry face the chances are that even though they are saying hello and telling us their name we probably won't want to speak to that person.

Smiles are a very important part of getting along with others.

Remind pupils of the rules for opening a conversation:

- Relax, take a deep breath and say encouraging things to yourself.

- Smile.

- Say 'Hi' to the person and tell them your name.

Pair and Share

Pupils complete Activity 15 which asks them to list the positive self-talk they can use before opening up a conversation.

- Pupils take turns with their partner to discuss the responses.

- Pupils complete a 'Pair and Share' evaluation.

Final Plenary

- Ask pupils to suggest specific times when they will. Practice opening up conversations during the week.

- Remind pupils that as with all new skills the more often they practice them, the easier it will be and the more often we have the courage to open up a conversation with someone new, we increase our chances of making a new friend to have fun with.

- Remind the pupils of the aims of the session and ask them to put their hand up if they consider that out of a score of ten they would give the session five or above for having achieved its aims.

Take Away Activities

- Practice the steps for opening up conversations with others during the week. Make a list of these times in the Friendship Log.

- Watch others who are friendly and notice how they open up conversations.

- Make a list of encouraging things you say to yourself in the Friendship Log.

Date:_____

Make a list of the encouraging things that you can say to yourself to open up a conversation.

P is for Persuasion   Poster 16

Please…

I would like you to………………………………………………

Do you think that…………………………………………………?

To sort this out we could…………………………………………

We could decide together………………………………………

Maybe this time we could………………………………………

Can I make a suggestion…………………………………………?

P is for Persuasion

Aims

○ To enable pupils to understand how to persuade others to change their minds.

○ To teach the skills of persuasion.

Whole Class Introduction

Explain to the class that persuasion means encouraging somebody to change their minds.

Ask pupils to give examples of times when they have wanted another person to change their mind. Scribe the examples.

Ask the pupils for examples of the sorts of things that we can do to get somebody else to change their mind.

Previous responses have included:

- Ask nicely.

- Say please.

- Explain why it is so important to you.

- Say that this won't happen all the time.

- Tell the person they are very kind.

- Give them a present.

- Tidy your bedroom.

Ask the class for two volunteers, one who will role play being a parent and the second a child who is persuading the parent to allow them to have a dog.

Ask the class for feedback. Encourage the class to discuss the effectiveness of the arguments. What was successful and what did not work? Vote on what the parent should decide.

Ask the pupils to role play a different situation. Pupils may either choose their own scenario or choose one from the following list which should be written on the board:

- Stay up late to watch TV.

- Stay for a sleep-over with a friend.

- Be given more pocket money.

- Stay out late at a disco.

Ask pupils to change roles and choose another scenario.

Pair and Share

Ask pupils to complete Activity 16 which asks the pupils to write about persuading a friend to go to the cinema instead of a museum.

- Pupils take turns with their partner to discuss the responses.

- Pupils complete a 'Pair and Share' evaluation.

Final Plenary

- Ask the pupils to reflect on the session and what they have learnt about being persuasive and how to go about encouraging somebody to change their mind.

- Remind the pupils of the aims of the session and ask them to put their hand up if they consider that out of a score of ten they would give the session five or above for having achieved its aims.

Take Away Activities

- Ask pupils to watch carefully for situations during the coming week where they spot that somebody is being persuasive. In the Friendship Log describe how that person is going about getting somebody to change their mind.

- Make a list of situations where you want to persuade somebody to change their mind in your Friendship Log.

- Write a short play about a person who wants to encourage another person to change their minds.

- Watch advertisements on the TV or at the cinema and think about what message the advertisements are trying to get across.

Date:_____

Your best friend wants you to go with her to a museum for her birthday treat. You want to go to see a new film. What can you say to persuade your friend to go to the cinema?

Dear

Advice for Quarrels

Stay Calm.

What is the problem?

Listen to the other's point of view.

Think about the choices you could make.

Make a good choice.

Aims

○ To enable pupils to recognise the behaviours that lead to quarrels.

○ To encourage pupils to practice the skills involved in negotiation.

Whole Class Introduction

Explain to the pupils that during this session we are going to be thinking about some of the behaviours that can lead us to not getting along with others and having quarrels and what we can do about this.

Ask the pupils to remember the last time they fell out with somebody and had a quarrel. Scribe their responses.

Reassure pupils that everybody has quarrels from time to time and that there are ways that quarrels can be sorted out. Explain to the class that it is important that they learn how to manage uncomfortable situations instead of getting into a quarrel. Emphasise to the pupils that they have control over their behaviour and that quarrels can be sorted out. The steps for sorting out quarrels are the same as for solving problems. If you know and follow the steps you can sort out quarrels in a friendly and sensible way.

- The first thing is to recognise when you are beginning to get angry or upset and stay calm. To help you do this you can take deep breaths, count to five or say something positive to yourself. Remember if you lose your temper, you may also lose your chance of sorting things out with the other person because they will get angry too.

- Secondly it is important to think carefully what the problem is.

- Thirdly listen carefully to the person's responses and think about why they might be feeling this way.

- Fourthly think about your choices.

  compromise
  speak calmly
  take turns
  say how you feel in a friendly way using 'I' talk not 'you' talk.

- Finally decide on your best choice and do it.

Discuss with the pupils the process of sorting out a quarrel using an example of a quarrel from the list generated by the pupils at the beginning of the session.

- What is the problem?

- What are your choices?

- What are the consequences of these choices?

- What is the best thing to do?

- Make a choice.

Explain to the class that there are things they should do and things they shouldn't do during a quarrel. Ask pupils to suggest what these may be?

Make a list of do's and don'ts from pupils' responses.

Previous responses have included:

Do	Don't
keep calm	*shout*
say something positive to yourself	*argue back*
think of some solutions to the problem	*be rude*
use 'I' talk.	*use 'you' talk.*

Pair and Share

Pupils complete Activity 17 which asks them to identify the correct sentence endings.

- Pupils take turns with their partner to discuss the responses.

- Pupils complete a 'Pair and Share' evaluation.

Final Plenary

- Ask pupils to think about what they have learnt in the session.

- Ask pupils to think about what they will do differently as a result of the session.

- Remind the pupils of the aims of the session and ask them to put their hand up if they consider that out of a score of ten they would give the session five or above for having achieved its aims.

Take Away Activities

- Watch for people having quarrels on TV or during films and think about how they behave. Make a record this in the Friendship Log.

- In the Friendship Log write a story or draw a picture about two people having a quarrel.

Date: _____

Quarrels can start very easily. At home it is easy to argue about what to watch on TV or with your friends about what game to play.

Draw a line to join each sentence with the correct ending.

If we are bowling and we
have to decide who goes
first we can...

Ask for help from
an adult.

My friend wants to see
one film and I want to
see another...

Listen to the others
point of view.

If there is a serious
quarrel in class
you can...

Get upset.

When you have a
quarrel with somebody
you may...

Toss a coin.

What are the good ways you use to settle quarrels?

A compliment is like a gift

Look at the person.

Say thank you.

Enjoy the compliment and feel good.

Aims

○ To enable pupils to understand that receiving a compliment can be difficult.

○ To practice receiving compliments in a positive way.

Whole Class Introduction

In this lesson we are going to be thinking about compliments again. You give someone a compliment, you smile, you wait to see the other person smile but sometimes you have to wait for a very long time. It is important to understand that for some people receiving compliments can make them feel very uncomfortable and they may act as if they don't care when somebody says something nice to them. Sometimes this is because they do not know what to say in return so they say nothing at all. This can be very uncomfortable for the person who is giving the compliment. Remember how in Session 3 we talked about how to pay somebody a compliment? In this lesson we are going to be thinking about the next step which is what to do when somebody gives you a compliment.

Since Session 3 we have been doing a very good job in this class of giving each other compliments. Think for a few moments about the last time somebody said something nice to you. What did you do? When you receive a compliment what do you think and what do you feel?

Previous responses have included:

- I said 'Thank you'.

- I sometimes think the person is making fun of me.

- I sometimes think the person is lying.

- I sometimes think that the person is trying to trick me or make me do something that I don't want to do.

- Compliments make me feel happy.

- I don't know what to say when somebody gives me a compliment.

Sometimes it can be very difficult for people to accept compliments. We can feel really embarrassed and not know what to say back. Let's think about how we feel in this class when we get a compliment.

Now I am going to ask you some questions and I want you to think about the answers and put your hand up if that has ever happened to you.

When you give somebody a compliment do they:

- Tell you that the compliment isn't true.

- Pretend that they haven't heard you.

- Tell you to get lost.

- Smile at you.

- Look very happy and say 'Thank you'.

The results of the survey will probably indicate that the pupils have mixed feelings about receiving compliments. It is important to emphasise to the class that receiving a compliment can sometimes be very awkward for us and we can feel uncomfortable.

We can all agree that sometimes things can go wrong with compliments. Listen to this story and think about what is happening?

There was a boy called Tom waiting at the bus stop outside the school. He had been late getting out of school and had missed the early bus. Tom knew that he had fifteen minutes to wait for the next bus so while he was waiting he decided to play Snakes on his mobile phone. Winston was also waiting at the same bus stop as Tom. He did not have a mobile phone but had been hoping his mum would buy him one for his birthday which was two weeks away. Now Winston's mum had been very ill and Winston knew that his mum would not be able to go to the shops to buy him a present. Mum would give him the money and send him to the shops with his big brother Nelson to buy the present. Winston watched Tom playing with his phone as they waited for the bus. Suddenly Winston remembered what his teacher had told him in school during a lesson about compliments. Winston's teacher had said if you notice something good about somebody and you want to get to know them pay them a compliment. Winston smiled at Tom and said 'That's a cool phone, where did you get it?' Tom suddenly became very angry and turned to Winston and said 'you think I stole this phone, get lost, leave me alone'. Winston was shocked and was very glad that he could see the bus coming round the corner. Winston made up his mind that he was going to sit as far away as possible from Tom when he got on the bus.

Now Winston wasn't being rude to Tom he was paying him a compliment so why did Tom respond the way he did? How do you think Winston felt when Tom reacted to his compliment in that way?

How do you think Tom was feeling in the story?

Some people tell us that they feel very shy and uncomfortable when they are given a compliment and they say that they do not want to hear what the person is saying to them and wish the person would just go away. A compliment can make both people feel uncomfortable. Some people think that a compliment is being used to trick them into doing something they don't want to do. Some people argue with the person who is giving them a compliment as if they want them to change their mind about saying something nice. In this lesson we are going to think about how to enjoy receiving a compliment without feeling embarrassed or uncomfortable.

We learnt that there are three rules for giving compliments and now we are going to think about three rules for receiving a compliment. This is important because we have learnt that hearing somebody say something nice about us can be very difficult. It can make us feel uncomfortable, embarrassed or even angry like Tom felt in the story.

These are the three things to remember when somebody gives you a compliment.

First, look at the person who is speaking to you. This is an important rule which we have learnt before: when somebody is talking to you it is important to look at them. Looking at them means we are listening to them. They know we are hearing them.

Secondly, while you are still looking at the person say thank you. You can say something else if you like but you don't have to. Be sure to say 'Thank You' clearly so the person can hear you, you can even pay the person a compliment back like 'That was kind of you to notice'

Thirdly enjoy the compliment and think about how good it feels when somebody notices you and says something positive about you.

Now let's think about how Tom could have reacted when Winston told him that he liked his phone.

Tom: *Thanks, yes it's great. I had it for my birthday.*

Winston: *It's my birthday soon and my mum said I can have a phone but I will have to go to the shop with my brother to buy it' cos my mum is ill.*

Tom: *My dad looked at a lot of shops before we got this one, I will tell you where you and your brother can go to get the best deal.*

Winston: *Thanks.*

Let's remind ourselves of the three rules for accepting a compliment:

1 Look at the person,

2 Say 'Thank you'

3 Feel good.

Pair and Share

Pupils complete Activity 18, which asks the pupils to consider how different people might respond to a compliment.

- Pupils take turns with their partner to discuss the responses.

- Pupils complete a 'Pair and Share' evaluation.

Final Plenary

- The teacher should ask the pupils to reflect upon the session and remind them that the aim of the lesson was to think about receiving compliments can sometimes be difficult and to learn the three rules for receiving compliments. Ask the class if anybody has anything to tell the class about what they learnt today.

- Finish the lesson by complimenting the class on how well they worked during this session and use the remaining time to play 'Compliments Carry-on'. Ask the class if anybody would like to volunteer to pay somebody in the class a compliment and remind the pupils that they must respond using the three rules of looking at the speaker, saying thank you and feeling good. Then that person chooses somebody else in the class to compliment. Ask the class to watch very carefully to make sure that the pupils who are giving compliments and those who are receiving them are following all the rules.

- At the end of the session remind the pupils that even though the lesson is over they should continue to pay each other compliments.

- Remind the pupils of the aims of the session and ask them to put their hand up if they consider that out of a score of ten they would give the session five or above for having achieved its aims.

Take Away Activities

- Suggest pupils record the compliments that they receive in their Friendship Log.

- Suggest the pupils keep a record of the times when they pay somebody a compliment and record the person's reaction to the compliment.

- Ask the pupils to create a list of words and phrases to use when they receive a compliment in their Friendship Log.

Date:_____

Think about what these children might say if you paid them a compliment. Write the words around them.

Johnny OK

Mary Not OK

Sorry

Saying sorry means that you are

Brave

Aims

○ **To raise pupils' awareness of the importance of saying sorry.**

○ **To help pupils practise when and how to say sorry.**

Whole Class Introduction

In this lesson we are going to talk about something that is sometimes very hard to do and this is saying 'I am sorry'.

Ask pupils to think about last time they said sorry to somebody and think about how they felt?

Explain to the class that sometimes when somebody gets angry with you and tells you lots of things that you don't want to hear, you know you ought to just say sorry and get all the upset over and done with but somehow the words 'I'm sorry' just won't seem to come out of your mouth. Now let's think about some of the reasons why it might be very hard to say sorry.

Previous responses have included:

- Haven't done anything wrong.

- I just don't want to talk to that person.

- I'm embarrassed.

- I feel frightened.

Saying sorry just means you are sorry. One hard thing about saying sorry is the feeling that if you say sorry or apologise for something it's like saying you are the one in the wrong. Saying sorry can sometimes feel like you are admitting that you are wrong and the other person is right. Saying sorry doesn't mean this, it just means you are sorry.

Ask the class if there is anybody willing to share a time when they were able to tell somebody they were sorry even though it was a very hard thing to do? If pupils are reluctant to talk it may be helpful for the teacher to start the discussion by giving a personal example of saying sorry when it was a very difficult thing to do.

Saying sorry means you are brave. It can be very scary to say I'm sorry because the other person might get very angry with you and tell you to clear off. When kids get older they start to get braver because they are learning to think about how other people are feeling not just how they are feeling themselves. It starts to be very important to them if the other person is angry or upset and they want to do something to help the person feel better. Saying 'I am sorry' can help the situation.

There are four steps which can make it easier for you to say I'm sorry.

1 Look at the person.

2 Say 'I'm sorry' in a clear voice.

3 Offer to do something that might make the person feel better.

4 Remember to feel good about yourself for being brave and thoughtful enough to say 'I'm sorry'. Tell yourself 'Well done'.

Don't forget that sometimes people can be very angry and may not want you to hear you say 'I'm sorry'. Don't worry the important thing is that you've said it. The person may just need some more cooling down time before they want to hear you say sorry. Later they will probably be very happy when they remember that you have said 'I'm sorry' to them.

Pair and Share

Pupils complete Activity 19 which asks them how they would say sorry in different situations.

- Pupils take turns with their partner to discuss the responses.

- Pupils complete a 'Pair and Share' evaluation.

Final Plenary

- Asks pupils to share with the class something new that they learnt during the lesson.

- Ask the pupils to describe what they will do differently as a result of the session.

- Remind the pupils of the aims of the session and ask them to put their hand up if they consider that out of a score of ten they would give the session five or above for having achieved its aims.

Take Away Activities

- Watch TV or films and notice when people are saying sorry to each other. Write or draw about this in your Friendship log.

- Write a story or draw a picture called 'I'm so sorry'.

- Make a list in your Friendship Log of the times when you say sorry to people.

Date:_____

Think how you would say sorry to the following people:

You have dropped paint on your mothers best coat. When she comes home you say,

You forgot your best friends birthday. Next time you meet them you say,

Samaya accused her brother of stealing her phone. She later found it under her bed. When her brother comes home she says,

Write about times when you have said sorry.

_____

_____

_____

_____

_____

_____

Turn Taking

Ask open questions

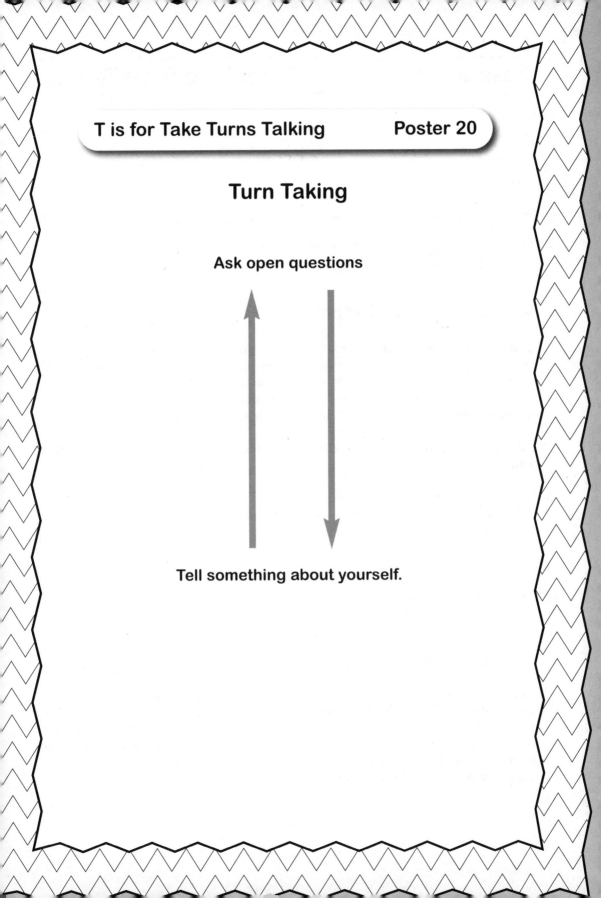

Tell something about yourself.

Aims

○ To teach pupils to take turns in conversations.

○ To enable pupils to practice basic conversational skills.

Whole Class Introduction

Explain to the class that if we want to find out what a new person is like, we have to talk to them. We have to ask them questions about themselves, listen carefully to their answers and then tell them something about ourselves too. This is called 'taking turns'. Taking turns is important because if one person does all the talking and does not listen the other person will usually not want to continue the conversation.

Ask pupils what sort of questions they think would be good to ask somebody if they wanted to get to know them?

Suggest to the pupils that some questions work better than others when you want to talk to somebody. Illustrate this by asking a variety closed questions that only require a 'yes' or 'no' response such as:

Are you in Year 6?

Do you like this school?

Do you play football?

Do you watch Eastenders?

Ask the pupils to think about whether these questions helped to make a good conversation? Did they help two people to talk together very well? Explain to the pupils that questions that can be answered with 'yes' or a 'no' are called 'closed' because they only need a very short answer. It can be very difficult to have an interesting and friendly conversation with 'closed' questions because the 'yes' or 'no' answers can make a conversation sound more like a quiz.

Now ask the class the following questions:

What sports do you like playing?

What are your favourite foods?

What music do you like to listen to?

Encourage the pupils to think about the answers to these questions; were the answers more interesting? Did the pupils enjoy listening to the answers? Explain to the pupils that asking a different kind of question, an 'open' question works better than asking 'closed' questions because they can get people really talking and they don't get stuck just saying 'yes' and 'no' to each other all the time.

Take a few minutes for the pupils to suggest some examples of open-ended questions or closed questions. Scribe each example and then ask the class to decide what type of question it is. When approximately twelve questions have been scribed ask the pupils what they notice about the questions?

Pupils may notice that closed questions usually start with words such as 'Do' and 'Are' and open-ended questions usually start with words that begin 'wh'. e.g. what, why, where, when.

Explain to pupils that another part of getting to know somebody is telling them something about ourselves. Ask pupils for suggestions as to what they could tell somebody about themselves. Scribe their responses.

Summarise the main points of the lesson:

If we want to get to know somebody we have to:

- Ask that person open questions.

- Tell that person something about yourself.

Pair and Share

Pupils should complete Activity 20 which asks them to consider the different responses open and closed questions generate.

- Pupils take turns with their partner to discuss the responses.

- Pupils complete a 'Pair and Share' evaluation.

Final Plenary

- Ask pupils to share with the class something new that they learnt from talking to their partner.

- At the end of this activity the teacher needs to praise the pupils for their contributions to the lesson and remind them to practice the rules for taking turns talking.

- Remind the pupils of the aims of the session and ask them to put their hand up if they consider that out of a score of ten they would give the session five or above for having achieved its aims.

Take Away Activities

- Ask pupils to listen carefully to the questions they hear during the week and decide whether they are open or closed questions. Make a list of open questions and closed questions in their Friendship Log.

- Ask pupils to practice asking open-ended questions especially when they are talking to somebody they do not know very well. Write about this activity in the Friendship Log.

- Suggest pupils listen carefully to interviews on the TV or radio and in their Friendship Log make a list of the questions the interviewer uses noting whether these are open or closed questions.

- Things about me. Make a list in the Friendship Log of all the things about yourself you could share with somebody new.

Date:_____

Ask your partner the following questions:

Closed	Open
Do you like sports?	Tell me about the sports that you like?
Do you listen to music?	What kind of music do you like?
Do you watch TV?	What do you like to do for fun?

Now tell your partner something about you.

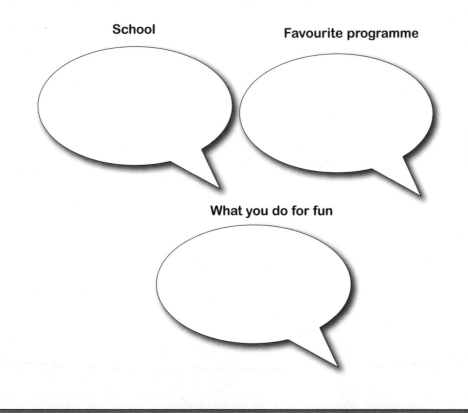

School

Favourite programme

What you do for fun

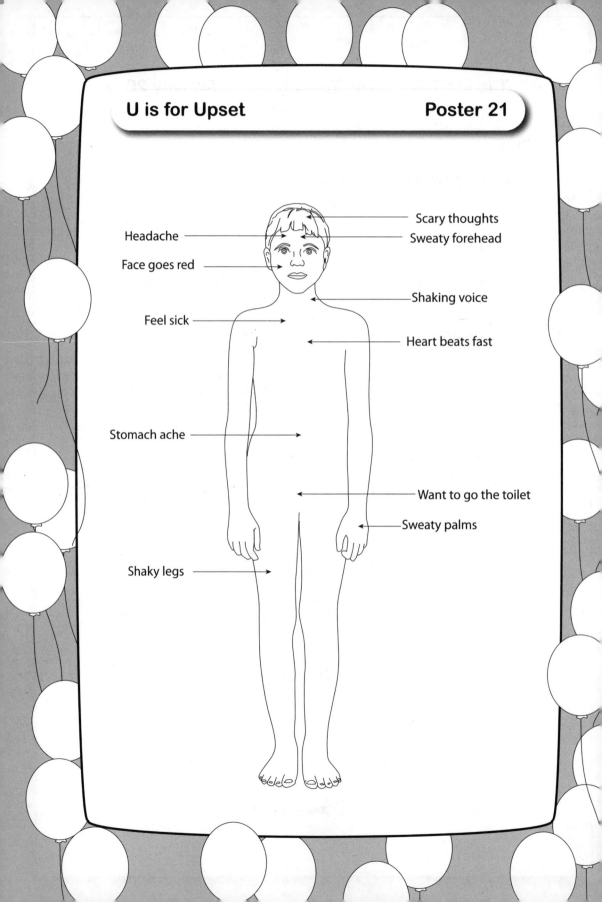

Aims

○ To enable pupils to identify the body clues that tell them they are beginning to feel upset.

○ To encourage pupils to make the link between what is happening to their bodies and difficult situations.

Whole Class Introduction

Explain to the class that this lesson is going to be about learning to recognise when we are feeling upset or worried. Explain that our body can give us clues or warning signs when we are beginning to feel upset. Ask pupils for examples of what they think these clues or warning signs may be. Emphasising that these clues can be different from person to person. Scribe pupils' responses on an enlarged version of Poster 21 which is an outline of the human body.

Previous examples have included:

- Headaches.

- Stomach aches.

- Wanting to go to the toilet often.

- Feeling sick.

- Blush.

- Want to be sick.

N.B.   It is important to be aware that if pupils give examples such as 'butterflies in my stomach' or 'I go red' this may be confusing and even disturbing for pupils with communication difficulties who are likely to interpret these terms literally. Pupils with hearing impairment may also not understand these terms and it is therefore important the teacher either encourages pupils to describe their symptoms more clearly or the takes the opportunity to clearly explain these terms to reduce alarm and so there is no confusion.

Explain to the pupils that our bodies give us clues when we are feeling upset because it wants us to relax and take it easy. We can see how important it is to stop ourselves feeling upset and worried by watching athletes on the TV or films. Before a race or competition we can often see athletes relax their bodies by stretching their muscles, shaking their arms and legs and taking slow, deep breaths. They do this to relax themselves and stop themselves being upset or worried about the race. Explain to the pupils that when we notice that we are feeling upset it is our body beginning to give us clues. It is important to take slow, deep breaths because this is a way of gaining control over our body, makes our heart beat slower and we feel less upset.

Pair and Share

Pupils complete Activity 21 which asks them to draw their body and label what happens when they get upset and worried.

- Pupils take turns with their partner to discuss the responses.

- Pupils complete a 'Pair and Share' evaluation.

Final Plenary

- Ask pupils for examples of things that they have learnt that they can do to stop themselves feeling upset.

- End the session by encouraging the pupils to spend a few minutes focusing on taking deep breaths in order to encourage feelings of well-being and relaxation.

- Remind the pupils of the aims of the session and ask them to put their hand up if they consider that out of a score of ten they would give the session five or above for having achieved its aims.

Take Away Activities

- Ask pupils to practice looking out for clues that they might be getting upset and practice ways of relaxing such as taking deep breaths.

- Suggest pupils keep a record of when this happens using the following prompts.

Date:_____

Body clues:_____

_____

What is happening to make me feel upset?_____

_____

What I did to relax?_____

_____

- Watch sport on the TV and notice how athletes prepare for games and races by stretching their muscles and practising deep breathing. Draw or write about this in your Friendship Log.

- Watch carefully for clues that tell you that other people especially your family or friends maybe getting upset. Write or draw about this in your Friendship Log.

Date:_____

Draw your body and add the things that happen to give you clues to show that you are feeling upset and worried.

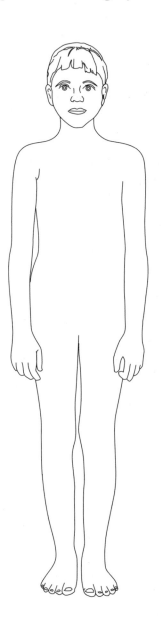

Saying thank you is an important way of showing people we value them.

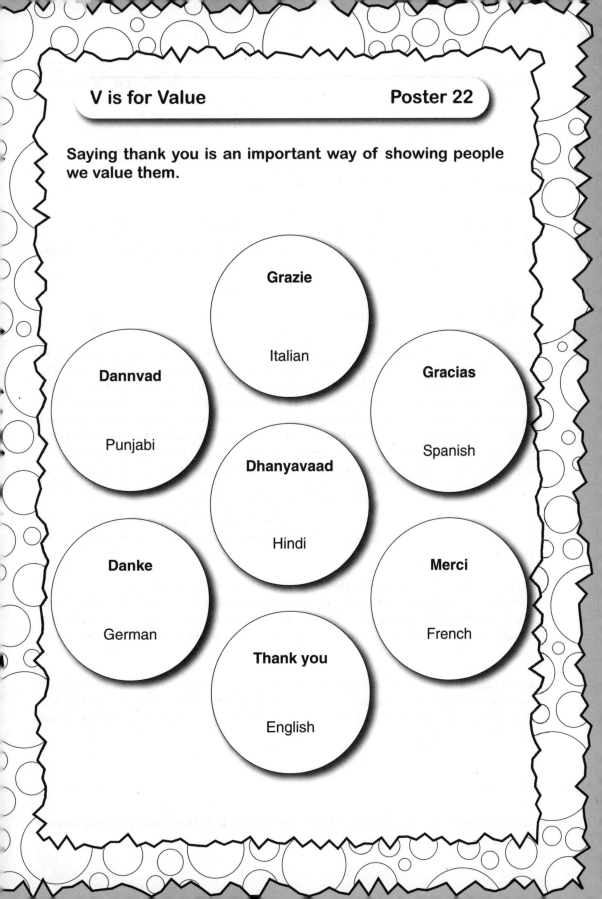

Grazie

Italian

Dannvad

Punjabi

Gracias

Spanish

Dhanyavaad

Hindi

Danke

German

Merci

French

Thank you

English

Aims

O   **To enable pupils to understand the importance of valuing others.**

O   **To encourage pupils to practice ways of showing that they value others.**

Whole Class Introduction

If you want to get along well with others and make friends the important thing to remember is to show people that you value them. How can you do this? By showing them attention and letting them know that you like them because of their special qualities. An important fact to learn in this programme is to always remember that people want to be valued by other people. This is part of being human and we all need to feel valued by others. If you can show others that you appreciate them just for being who they are then they will feel valued by you. If you let people know that you appreciate them they will relax and appreciate you and the other people around them more in return. Sometimes this is called 'the ripple effect'. You show somebody that you value them and they go on their way feeling good about themselves and more cheerful and in turn show their appreciation to somebody else. No matter what small thing you do to make others feel good the ripples of your action will affect many other people.

Let's start with the people we already know. You don't have to wait until they do something special for you before you can let them know how much you value them. Think about all the people already in your life who do things for you but who you usually take for granted and think about what you can do to show them you value them?

Remember *everybody* has something to offer, if you don't at first notice something you value about a person think again. If you can find somebody's good points they will become happier and they will like you more too because you have made them feel good about themselves.

Pair and Share

Pupils complete Activity 22 which asks them to show how they value various elements of their life.

- Pupils take turns with their partner to discuss the responses.

- Pupils complete a 'Pair and Share' evaluation.

Final Plenary

- Ask pupils to think about what they have learnt from the session.

- Remind the pupils of the aims of the session and ask them to reflect on how well they consider these have been met.

- Remind the pupils of the aims of the session and ask them to put their hand up if they consider that out of a score of ten they would give the session five or above for having achieved its aims.

Take Away Activities

- Think about the people in your life and in your Friendship Log make a list of the ways that you can let them know you value them.

- While you are watching TV or films think about how people are showing that they value each other and write about this in your Friendship Log.

Date:_____

How can you show you value:

Your family: **Your friends:**

_____   _____

_____   _____

_____   _____

_____   _____

_____   _____

Your neighbours: **Your pet:**

_____   _____

_____   _____

_____   _____

_____   _____

_____   _____

Your school: **Your planet:**

_____   _____

_____   _____

_____   _____

_____   _____

_____   _____

Win/Win

- Nobody is hurt.

- An acceptable solution is found.

- Both people respect each other and themselves.

Aims

○ To introduce pupils to a Win/Win problem solving process.

○ To enable pupils to practice Win/Win problem solving to deal with specific conflicts.

Whole Class Introduction

Explain to the pupils that Win/Win means that both people sort out a problem or disagreement and in the end they both feel good about how things have turned out.

Ask pupils to give examples of times when they have managed to sort out a problem with somebody so that they both ended up feeling good about things.

Ask pupils why they think they were successful in sorting things out?

Explain to the class that in order to get to Win/Win both people must be willing to co-operate with each other and talk to each other so that they can sort things out.

Explain to the pupils that there are steps that they can use to get to Win/Win.

- It is important to say what the problem is or ask for what you want in a clear way. It is important to keep calm and look at the person. If you get angry the other person will get angry too. Explain how you feel and what worries you about using 'I' messages. Speak in a calm voice and use polite body language. Look at the person. Do not fold your arms or frown at the person.

- It is important to listen really carefully to what the other person is saying and don't interrupt. Look for 'body talk' clues to help you.

- Think very carefully about what the person is saying and why they may be feeling that way. If you don't understand what the person is saying ask for more information in a kind, not in an angry voice. You could say: 'I'm sorry I don't understand what you are saying, could you explain to me what you are saying?'

- Clarify the problem together and think about both sides of the misunderstanding.

- Brainstorm solutions.

- Agree on what to do.

- If you can't agree on a solution arrange to talk again in a few days.

Pair and Share

Pupils complete Activity 23 which asks them to indicate that they understand what happens in conflicts.

- Pupils take turns with their partner to discuss the responses.

- Pupils complete a 'Pair and Share' evaluation.

Final Plenary

- Ask pupils to share something new they have learnt from the session.

- Ask the pupils to describe what they will do differently as a result of the session.

- Remind the pupils of the aims of the session and ask them to put their hand up if they consider that out of a score of ten they would give the session five or above for having achieved its aims

Take Away Activities

- Suggest pupils design a poster for the Friendship Log called 'Win/Win'.

- Watch TV or films and notice when people get to a win/win situation. Write about this in the Friendship Log.

- Look for pictures in newspapers and magazines of people when they are in a win/win situation. Cut out the pictures and put them in the Friendship Log. Make a title for each picture.

Date:_____

Draw a line to indicate the outcome.

	☺ ☹
One person gets hurt	Win/Lose

	☺ ☺
Both people find a solution...................	Win/Win

	☹ ☹
Neither person gets their way................	Lose/Lose

	☺ ☺
Both people feel OK..............................	Win/Win

	☹ ☹
Both people continue arguing...............	Lose/Lose

	☺ ☹
One person runs away crying...............	Win/Lose

Draw a picture or write about a win/win situation.

It's not what you say.

It's the way that you say it.

Take Away Activities

- Suggest pupils collect for their Friendship Log pictures from magazines and newspapers to illustrate a wide range of facial expressions and body language.

- Ask pupils to watch an episode of their favourite soap with the volume off so that they have to guess what is happening by watching how the characters behave. Record their findings in the Friendship Log.

Date:_____

What have you learnt?

What will you do next?

It's up to you?

Resources

- Allow approximately 45 minutes to run the session.

- A4 copies of the final evaluative activity for each pupil.

- Pens, pencils, rubbers, sharpeners, etc.

- Friendship Logs.

This session takes the form of an end of programme review and provides an opportunity for pupils to focus individually on what they have learnt during the programme. Each pupil will complete a final evaluative activity. This exercise will provide each individual with an overview of the skills they have learnt throughout the programme and involves the pupils awarding themselves a score out of ten for the development that they consider that they have made in each the core skills and concepts that have taught in the programme. It will be necessary to emphasise to pupils the importance of completing the activity as honestly as possible so that they have a realistic knowledge of how much they have understood the various component parts of the programme.

As part of this exercise pupils are then asked to formulate a series of positive statements which reflect their own progress and achievement. These can include:

- I can pay compliments to my friends.

- I am better at knowing how other people are feeling.

Pupils are also asked to highlight three areas which they would like to continue to work on.

Target Setting

This activity can also be used to highlight any areas or specific skills that pupils may still need to work on. Some pupils may want to formulate specific targets for themselves and teachers may wish to encourage this process in order to generate appropriate targets for their individual education plans (IEPs).

Time permitting, pupils should be encouraged to complete their Learning Logs.

Final Plenary

- Remind the pupils that the next session will take the form of a party to celebrate all they have learnt during the programme.

- Suggest that the pupils may wish to bring snacks and games to play for their party.

Take Away Activities

- Suggest the pupils may wish to complete their Friendship Log before the final session.

Y is for You

Each of the statements in this quiz will be about something you have learnt about making friends. Below each statement are the numbers 1–10.

Think about each statement and then choose one number that you think matches how you feel.

Circle number 1 – if you never do what the statement says. asks.

Circle number 5 – if you sometimes do it.

Circle number 10 – if you always do it.

Use the other numbers in between if you think that they who best where you are.

Remember that there are no right or wrong answers to these statements. Circle the way you really feel about each one.

1. **I can listen to someone who is talking to me.**

    1   2   3   4   5   6   7   8   9   10

2. **I can ask for help in a friendly way when I need to.**

    1   2   3   4   5   6   7   8   9   10

3. **I can say thank you to people when they have done something for me.**

    1   2   3   4   5   6   7   8   9   10

4. I can open up talks with people.

    1   2   3   4   5   6   7   8   9   10

5. I can ask to join in a game or activity in a friendly way.

    1   2   3   4   5   6   7   8   9   10

6. I can ask someone to help me.

    1   2   3   4   5   6   7   8   9   10

7. I can tell others that I like something about them or say something nice that they have done for me or somebody else.

    1   2   3   4   5   6   7   8   9   10

8. When someone says that they like something about me I believe what they say and say, 'Thank you.'

    1   2   3   4   5   6   7   8   9   10

9. I can say I'm sorry after I don something wrong.

    1   2   3   4   5   6   7   8   9   10

10. I can let others know what I am feeling and do it in a good way.

    1   2   3   4   5   6   7   8   9   10

11. When someone has a problem I can let them know that I understand how they feel.

    1   2   3   4   5   6   7   8   9   10

12. When I am in a bad mood I can manage it in ways that won't hurt other people.

    1   2   3   4   5   6   7   8   9   10

13. I let others know that I value them.

    1   2   3   4   5   6   7   8   9   10

14. I can say good things to myself to make me feel better.

    1   2   3   4   5   6   7   8   9   10

15. I can think about different ways of dealing with a problem.

    1   2   3   4   5   6   7   8   9   10

16. When I don't agree with somebody we can work out a plan to make both of us happy.

    1   2   3   4   5   6   7   8   9   10

17. I can tell others calmly when they have caused a problem for me.

    1   2   3   4   5   6   7   8   9   10

18. I can tell others something good about they they played a game.

    1   2   3   4   5   6   7   8   9   10

19. If I have been left out I can keep calm and do things in a good way to make myself feel better.

    1   2   3   4   5   6   7   8   9   10

20. **When a group of kids want me to do something that may get me in trouble, I can say, 'No.'**

    1   2   3   4   5   6   7   8   9   10

21. **I can tell the truth about what I have done even if I might get into trouble.**

    1   2   3   4   5   6   7   8   9   10

Three positive statements about me:

1. _____

2. _____

3. _____

Three things I'm working at to improve:

1. _____

2. _____

3. _____

Z is for Zest for Living

Resources

- Allow approximately 45 minutes to run the session.

- Photocopies of the Certificate of the completion of the programme for each pupil signed and dated by the teacher and head teacher.

- Friendship Logs.

- Refreshments, music, games, as required.

The final session of the programme will not follow the usual format but will be a celebration session to mark the end of the programme. Pupils should be encouraged in preparation for this final session to think about what games and activities they would like to bring along.

These should be awarded to pupils during the session in recognition that they have completed the programme. Teachers may wish to ask the headteacher to sign and present the certificates.

Pupils should be reminded that this celebratory session is an opportunity for pupils to enjoy each other's company and practice the friendship skills that they have learnt throughout the programme.

Staff therefore may like to use the session as an opportunity to observe pupils' progress with regard to their ability to get along with others.

The areas to focus on will include the pupils' ability to:

- Listen to each other.

- Greet each other appropriately.

- Take turns in conversations and games.

- Ensure nobody is left out.

- Pay appropriate compliments to each other.

- Receive compliments appropriately.

- Welcome guests appropriately.

Enjoy the celebration.

How to make friends

This is to certify that

has attended this course and has learnt how to get

along with others and make friends

Signed: _____

Course Leader

Signed: _____

Head Teacher

Date: _____